The Art of War on Terror

Triumphing over Political Islam
and the Axis of Jihad

Printed in the United States of America

ISBN-10: 0-9794704-0-4

ISBN-13: 978-0-9794704-0-0

For 10 or more copies of this book contact:
www.moorthymuthuswamy.com

We can't be consumed by our petty differences anymore

We will be united in our common interests

You will once again be fighting for our freedom—not from tyranny, oppression or persecution, but from annihilation

We are fighting for our right to live—to exist!

We are going to survive!

Portions of a speech delivered before launching the decisive battle to defeat and destroy alien invaders (from *Independence Day*—a 1996 Hollywood blockbuster movie)

THE ART OF WAR ON TERROR

Contents

Contents

Preface

Reverses in Iraq and Afghanistan signify that America is on the retreat. We have nowhere to run. Jihadis will come to us. Left alone, radical Islam is not a containable problem. It will stop at nothing less than destruction of civilization as we know it. Radicals have a clear focus: the anchor state of civilization—America—must be brought to its knees; its economic and military capability must be significantly destroyed. Pressure is mounting on America and its military with the economic toll of the terror war already close to a trillion dollars thus far and over 6000 civilians and military personnel killed and several tens of thousands injured.

The quick and unprecedented victory of America-led coalition forces over Iraq has shown that Islamic states are lacking in conventional military might. However, through proxies, radical Islamic states have imposed a strategically effective terror war. Now more radical states are at the threshold of acquiring nuclear weapon capability.

This is a serious threat. Having weathered Nazis and countless invaders, portions of Europe face the probability of being overrun demographically by Muslim radicals. Among the states at the border of Islam, the lands of Israel and India are staring at the possibility of an Islamic conquest.

The up-to-date and extensive information required for conducting research—the so-called virtual library—is just a touch of a key away on the Internet. Indeed, the advent of the Internet has made it possible to develop a multidisciplinary approach to solving these problems, or even to win the war on terror.

There is a need for a scientific point of view in discrediting doctrines that tell believers to kill unbelievers. When so many nations' or societies' survival is at stake, especially when the enemy is a proven genocidal one who obeys no rules, problem-solving should take center-stage. This is something that traditional policy advising institutions, used to thinking in terms of diplomacy, military or a combination thereof, find it not easy to understand. The need to solve the radical Islamic problem is not lost on world leaders. President George Bush, for one, notes this as the "inescapable calling of our generation".[1]

I have moved away from using the term "radical Islam" to identify the enemy. The enemy is really the political Islamic movement; radical Islam is one subset of this political movement, one that has the objective of achieving unbeliever "conquest". Contrary to conventionally held beliefs, which hold that the radical Islamic movement that is represented by the likes of Al-Qaeda is an independent, stateless entity, this book develops the view of a movement that is thriving due to the continued sponsorship of mainly three nations and their citizens. These nations are Saudi Arabia, Pakistan, and Iran, and they are introduced in this book as the "Axis of Jihad". Incriminating data on axis nations is discussed here with the aim of developing a sense of grievance in victim nations. It is argued that the main reason for the limited headway that has been achieved thus far in the war on terror is due to America's and its allies' inability to effectively go after the axis of jihad nations and the nodes of social network in Muslim communities spawning terror.

This book discusses the ways in which America could execute an innovative multinational terror war policy without directly occupying jihad-sponsoring nations. For a successful counter-offensive against political Islam, there is a need to build and pursue crimes-against-humanity charges against axis of jihad nations, and to discredit the standing of Saudi Arabia—the nation most responsible for creating and sustaining the terror unleashed on unbelievers. A framework is put together in this book by identifying political Islam's theological weaknesses and exploiting them. Putting on the hat of a scientist, I give arguments based upon science and common sense to discredit the theology that Islamists use to justify jihad.

As an American-trained nuclear physicist, I can inform readers that nuclear bomb-making physics and technology is a thing of yester-year. Determined Muslim states will acquire nuclear bombs, as Pakistan has already demonstrated. In the near future, America, Israel, and India will be their primary targets. It is going to require more than military capability to dissuade Muslim radicals from using nukes on us. This topic is discussed here.

India is a nation that has long been ravaged by waves of Muslim invasions and that had been ruled by Muslim kings for over 500 years. It is also a nation that was divided on the basis of Islam only 60 years ago—and is yet seen by Islamists as having escaped Islamic control. All available evidence points to a concerted and ongoing effort to systematically destroy India and bring it under the Islamic fold. This is a daring, high-risk adventure against a nation of over one billion people, of which 850 million are non-Muslims. Amazingly, Islamists are making headway, and the siege of India by political Islam is intensifying, despite the current economic resurgence. The project conquest-India has a some big name backers—nation states whose passion is Islamic conquest. A study of political Islam in the Indian context offers America and others a wealth of data and insight into how the enemy operates and what is yet to come. This data and analysis, which is not yet widely known even to experts, should be useful, as we will see, in developing policy measures, including those geared toward preemption. A cornered India and its 850 million non-Muslim population offers an overstretched America the possibility of taking war to the jihadis and their sponsoring states.

Having fallen behind western societies in civilizational advancement (which rules out using Muslim "achievement" to impress and convince unbelievers to embrace Islam) but endowed with vast resources and a passion for conquest, political Islam's goal of worldwide conquest could be achieved only through a multi-front terror war, aimed at civilians and at making the cost unbearable for its enemies. We will note in this book that this constant pattern of terrorizing unbeliever populations is the most important way of achieving Islamic conquest. Hence, the name "War on Terror," used to define a multi-front war waged to neutralize political Islam, is quite an appropriate one.

Any such terror war requires committed adherents and an ideology that is perceived by many as being all-encompassing. The reader may be surprised to discover in these pages that nations with a medieval outlook could wage a fairly sophisticated jihad on unsuspecting and powerful nations. The framework presented in this book—compartmentalizing the problem and identifying enemy's weaknesses—could be considered a general outline for winning a terror war.

This book doesn't call for whole scale war on Muslims or for restriction of their individual rights. But it suggests how this war could be fought predominantly on ideological and political grounds. A survival problem of this magnitude requires an involved public. With that in mind, it is hoped that this book will make easy reading for non-experts.

Over the years the author has benefited from discussions with many people. Due to circumstances he is forced to be discreet in acknowledging their contributions.

Chapter One

What Went Wrong?

Even the most sanguine optimist couldn't deny that the war on terror, as manifested by extensive American and allied military engagements abroad (i.e., in Iraq and Afghanistan) is not proceeding well.[2,3] A more realistic view is that America is losing both strategically and militarily in both these theaters of operation. With recruitment apparently robust, radical Islam appears to be as strong as ever. This means that America-hating jihadis are continually produced in large numbers. This may point to the reality of the situation: the so-called pro-American regimes in some Islamic nations are not effective in countering jihad. Clearly, America needs a coherent new strategy to win the war on terror.

Five years in, the military expenses associated with the terror war alone may have cost at least as much as the Vietnam War—about 500 billion dollars.[4] There have been extensive other economic costs and internal security expenses as well.

North Korea and Iran are flexing their nuclear muscles, and a truly strategic and economic challenge to America is emerging from China in the not-so-near future. This China challenge far exceeds the one posed by the former Soviet Union.

Resurgent Political Islam

America has been the most dominant nation of the past century, especially after the Second World War. Understandably, until the last part of 20th century, western politicians and strategic experts came to view Islamic civilization as a struggling one, not a strategic threat at all.

Until recently many Islamic nations had been under the control of western colonizers. Due to this fact, little effort had been made by the westerners to understand the religious and political underpinnings of Islam. Yet Islam had been an expanding power until at least the 18th century, with a long history of conflict with Christianity, the majority religion in the West.

From a classical western view, in order for Islam to become a strategic threat, Muslim nations must first build their economies and industrial infrastructure to the point that they are comparable to those of the West, which would take many decades. For instance, Nazi Germany and Imperial Japan had become threats in 1930s because they had economies and industrial know-how that were comparable to those of the Allies. But radical Islamists have shown that, by influencing a vast majority of Muslim civilians globally and by converting many of them into foot-soldiers, they can become a strategic threat to the western civilization. In other words, they can overcome the deficiency of not being classical military powers. The proliferation of AK-47 assault rifles and bomb-making technology have made terror acts easier to execute and costlier to prevent.

Seen through the context of the Islamic trilogy—consisting of the Koran, Hadith and Sira—political Islam dominates over spiritual Islam (Chapter Two).[5] Hence Islam itself has a dominant political flavor to it. There is an internal component of political Islam, as it governs the kind of life and political system to which Muslims should adhere. But the internal politics of Islam and its legal code, called *sharia,* do not provide a way of setting up a modern state, for the obvious reason that it is an unchanged document that was written over a thousand years ago. Hence the economic and social aspirations of Muslims have gone unfulfilled, with rising expectations fueled by television and movies from the west and the east. However, the needed focus or a missing mission in the internal component is provided by the external one: conquest of "unbelievers," or non-Muslims. Political Islam concerns those of us who do not believe in its tenets, as it commands Muslims to conquer the world for Islam.

With other religions, when disciples' aspirations went unfulfilled, introspection resulted and it led to a reform of religious practices. However, as is discussed in the next chapter, one aspect of Islam that is unique is that whenever Muslims felt they had fallen behind, the most vocal voices were calling for Muslims to embrace even more retrogressive practices of political Islam. These practices include literal interpretations of the Islamic trilogy and the importance of conquest through jihad, rather than reform (i.e., the

17

reinterpretation of scriptures in a contemporary way and the downgrading of the importance given to them). The fundamentalists assert that once the whole world is Islamized everyone will feel fulfilled and be at peace with one another. Of course, fundamentalists may or may not realize the inconvenient reality that even in Islamic nations, different schools of religious thought are in conflict with each other.

In other words, inner political Islam is keeping Muslims from providing a better future for themselves and their families and the external political Islam commands them to wage jihad. Thus the increasingly accepted view is that the agenda set by political Islam is spawning terrorism.

The doctrine of jihad is the most important tool political Islam uses to assert its influence and achieve its vision. In general, the term jihad can be used to describe two concepts: there is an inner struggle, called "greater jihad," whose aim is to please the almighty God, and then there is "lesser jihad," which is external warfare aimed at conquest of land belonging to unbelievers and the imposition of Islam on its inhabitants. In Bukhari Hadith, the most respected of Hadiths, 97 percent of the jihad references are about war and 3 percent are about the inner struggle, showing that from a practical perspective lesser jihad is more important.[5]

In this book the word jihad is taken to mean the dominant form, the lesser jihad. This is the jihad Muslim extremists, radicals or jihadis—practitioners of jihad—mean in their discourse. Armed warfare imposed on unbelievers is one form of jihad. More generally, jihad should be understood as a struggle that uses every means possible to achieve the goal of Islamic conquest. The doctrine of jihad is used by political Islam to achieve conquest. Muslims who pursue political Islam's goals include activists—jihadis, radicals, extremists—and non-activist ordinary Muslims who identify with and sponsor actual activists. With this in mind, we can see that even though many ordinary Muslims are busy etching out a living, without their support political Islam's vision of Islamic conquest would be a non-starter. In this context the main goal of winning the war on terror can be defined as the negation of the support political Islam receives from Muslim public and sponsoring nations.

We will use the term "political Islam" to denote as the ideology we are fighting. This may be the first necessary step towards identifying the enemy correctly and coming up with a coherent policy response.

The majority of the Muslims associate the trilogy with all of the necessary information for leading a complete life.[6] This interpretation has made it difficult for Muslim nations to adapt new ideas and evolve, and especially to compete with the western world, which in the last several hundred years led the industrial revolution that is considered the basis for the modern world. The industrial revolution shifted wealth and power to the nations with industrial know-how. This put most Muslim nations at a disadvantage until huge deposits of petroleum were found in many Middle East nations, including Saudi Arabia, the birth nation of Islam's founder Mohammed.

Regardless of how predisposed a theology or an ideology is toward a certain outlook, such as conquest, it has to have committed and resourceful backers to become influential. In Saudi Arabia, political Islam has found a passionate backer. The enormous oil wealth of the country gave Saudis an opportunity to reinvigorate expansionist designs of political Islam. By many accounts, since the mid-

1970s, Saudi Arabia alone is said to have spent well over 85-90 billion dollars (strictly through official channels) on spreading Wahhabi-version of Islamic teachings to Sunni Muslim populations around the world.[7] It is also a tradition for Muslims in all walks of life to fund propagation of Islam.

There is every reason for Saudi Arabia to promote Wahhabism—i.e., to promote a political agenda of Saudi Arabia, cloaked as religion. Because Islam originated in Saudi Arabia, a nation under Wahhabi-ideological spell creates a civilization subservient to Saudi Arabia. During the early 1900s the Hyderabad Nawab (or the King) in India had periodically sent allowances to the Saudi royal family. With oil yet to be found, these allowances were an important source of funding for the royals.[8] Hence, it is not unreasonable for Saudi Arabia to invest in conquest and to expect a payoff later—in the form of subsidies from better-off Muslim nations, once oil revenues dry out in about a hundred years.

With a long and successful history of conquest and deeply Wahhabi, Saudi Arabia is unlikely to put to good use the free wealth it got in the form of oil revenues. From a traditional Wahhabi view, all useful knowledge is in the Islamic trilogy. By implication, there is really no useful knowledge in modern science; besides, science is associated with the "infidel" or "Christian" western world. Even within Saudi Arabia, education is tilted towards Islamic history and less towards modern literature or science.[9] Saudi Arabia has more than enough wealth to buy or pay for both skilled and unskilled guest workers, and their population in Saudi Arabia reflects this reality. When the call for jihad came from Soviet-occupied Afghanistan, the Saudi Arabian regime and society were more than prepared to assist a popular jihad.

An alternate and competing Islamic school of thought is Shiite Islam, which is distinguished from Sunni Islam. These two sects have bloody political differences dating back almost to the immediate aftermath of Mohammed's death. Iran, the most populous Shiite-dominant country, found itself awash with petroleum reserves. It also joined the movement of Islamic conquest in 1980s by spending its wealth to influence Shiite groups around the globe toward jihad.

Pakistan is the first Muslim nation to be carved out of a non-Muslim majority nation, as it was partitioned from British-ruled India in 1947. As the torchbearer for Islam in South Asia, Pakistan sees the largest nation in the region, non-Muslim-majority India, as the stumbling block for extending Islamic boundaries. Although Sunni-majority Pakistan was frustrated by its smaller size and lack of resources, it has an extensive track record of jihad dating back to 1947. Even without Saudi funding, between 1947-1980, Pakistan was a standout nation in terms of selective killings of non-Muslims or their displacement as part of a jihad. Generous jihad funding from Saudi Arabia (which is also predominantly Sunni) since the mid-1970s has made Pakistan even more powerful.

Perhaps more than any other Islamic nation, Pakistan has acted as a collaborator for Saudi Arabia and a translator of jihad plans into action; it has provided logistics, training and know-how for jihadist movements around the world. For instance, aided by Saudi Arabia, the Afghan Taliban was Pakistan's creation. There is also a suspicion that Saudi

Arabia has been heavily financing Pakistan's nuclear program for mutual benefit.[10]

The Soviet occupation of Islamic Afghanistan was used to build jihad fervor in many Islamic nations. This occupation also attracted holy warriors from many Islamic nations, including Egypt; this also includes Pakistan, the eventual base for anti-Soviet jihad. The Soviets found the occupation untenable because political Islam was entrenched in the minds of Afghans and because a relentless and resourceful enemy kept coming at them from Pakistan. After the Soviet retreat, an Afghan faction called the "Taliban" consolidated power. The Taliban consisted of former students from Pakistani *madarasas* (Muslim religious schools) and was the brainchild of Pakistani intelligence—specifically, the Inter-Services Intelligence (ISI).[11]

One unfortunate side product of the Soviet-Afghan war was the jihadist training of nationals from many Islamic nations. Upon returning home, many of these jihadis set about establishing terror cells with the aim of overthrowing existing governments that they saw as un-Islamic. As a result, instabilities were being created in many Muslim nations, such as Egypt, Saudi Arabia, and Pakistan. A band of Arab Islamic radicals, including Osama Bin Laden and his cohorts, decided to stay back in Afghanistan and use it as a base for jihad against unbelievers. Bin Laden's group, Al-Qaeda, operated in Taliban-ruled Afghanistan.

The attack on the World Trade Center in 1992 by Islamic radicals associated with Al-Qaeda should have served as a wake up call for America. In retrospect, we understand why it didn't. There were no easy options in dealing with Taliban or Al-Qaeda; Pakistan was not helpful. The Soviet imbroglio in Afghanistan was fresh in American minds. Also, Bin Laden's vision of war against unbelievers either was not clearly understood or was seen as being overly ambitious. An American attack on Taliban was seen as having potential for creating further instabilities in Islamic world and make America even more unpopular. However, the dominant reason was that political Islam, especially the version represented by Bin Laden's group, was seen as lacking the ability to strategically hurt America. "Militant or radical Islam" was seen as a transient phenomenon, one that had been created by the Afghan war and that was soon to die out.

But attacks on American interests that were attributed to Al-Qaeda were increasing in sophistication. Bin Laden was systematically escalating his rhetoric as well. His edict justifying killings of American civilians was made in 1998. Just before the African embassy bombings, the CIA looked into the possibility of capturing Bin Laden in Afghanistan, but eventually dropped the plan, as it was unsure of its success and worried about the casualties and their implications both in America and in the Islamic world.[12] The 1998 simultaneous American embassy bombings in Africa did wake the Clinton administration up. It responded with cruise missile strikes on Bin Laden's camps, but failed to kill him. According to the 9/11 Commission, officials in Washington suspected that Bin Laden or the Taliban might have received advance warning from Pakistani officials.[13] Then came the attack on Destroyer USS Cole. Soon after the attack the Bush administration took office and was notified of the evidence implicating Al-Qaeda. Condoleezza Rice, who at the time was National Security Advisor, told the 9/11 Commission that the President did not want to respond to Al-Qaeda one attack at a time. Instead, the administration apparently began to work on a "new strategy" to eliminate Al-Qaeda.[13]

American efforts were not successful for one main reason: America did not understand the new enemy. America had defeated the former Soviet Union, the old enemy, in a protracted struggle spread over four decades. The new enemy, political Islam, is very different from the old one; the new one fights in the name of God and the former abhors the very concept of God. A godless enemy such as the Soviet Union was easy to ostracize in an America led to believe that religion and God are constructive influences. For a nation founded on religious freedom, America seems to view religion as a constructive influence, and this has created significant complications in policymaking and in understanding the new enemy. There was another problem: America helped to create the jihad fervor through recruitment and training against the Soviet Union's occupation of Afghanistan.

For decades, the established American strategic know-how had been tuned to dealing with Soviet Communism. Hence there was little institutionalized knowledge of political Islam that the policy makers could rely upon. Also, heavy dependence on imported oil from nations that have long sponsored political Islam has not helped. A non-religious Soviet Union was amenable to rational discussion and accommodation, however difficult it might be. But jihadis blindly follow ancient scriptures and their outdated interpretations, and are not open to accommodation. Importantly, jihadis want nothing less than submission and conversion of America into Islam. Many radical Muslim leaders, such as Iran's Mahmoud Ahmadinejad, are even openly apocalyptic.

When it quickly became apparent that Al-Qaeda was behind 9/11 attacks, the Afghanistan invasion was inevitable. There was also considerable empathy and worldwide support for America in this invasion endeavor. A vastly superior American military invaded Afghanistan and quickly drove away both the Taliban and Al-Qaeda from power, with the help of anti-Taliban Northern Alliance. It now appears that poor military tactics allowed the toppled Al-Qaeda and Taliban leadership to escape to Pakistan.[14] There is no question that the capture or death of Bin Laden at American hands would have instilled fear in the minds of jihadis.

But Bin Laden, Al-Qaeda or the Taliban is just a symptom or proxy of a resurging political Islamic movement sponsored and nurtured by powerful entities in Saudi Arabia and Pakistan. Similarly, Hizbollah is sponsored by Shiite Iran. The problem with American strategy in the war on terror is its focus on the proxies and relative lack of focus on confronting and neutralizing its sponsors.

Taliban or Al-Qaeda were Proxies

Throughout the 1990s, jihadis had strong backing in the Middle East. Indeed, funds flowed generously, with most there viewing the Afghan Taliban regime as a virtuous Islamic government. In addition to Pakistan, the Taliban-controlled Afghanistan was recognized also by Saudi Arabia and the United Arab Emirates. Several reports trace the continued funding of Al-Qaeda to Saudi Arabia. A Canadian intelligence report concluded that Saudi charities funnel $1 to $2 million per month to the organization, while the Council on Foreign

Relations task force described Saudi individuals and charities as "the most important source of funds for Al-Qaeda" and deplored Saudis' turning "a blind eye" to this activity. Several principal financial backers of Al-Qaeda, most of them wealthy Saudis, were described as "the check writers."[15] While Al-Qaeda may not have been directly controlled by Saudi Arabia, it no doubt shared many Saudi aspirations. Hence it found a certain level of acceptance among the Saudi ruling elite and the public.

The Saudi government had been the principal financial backer of Afghanistan's fundamentalist Taliban movement since at least 1996. The Taliban not only had strong backing among the public in Pakistan, but ISI was at the forefront of sponsoring and aiding the Taliban. Fuel, arms, ammunition and even advice came from Pakistan.[16] The *madarasa*-educated, semi-illiterate Taliban leadership didn't have the experience in running the nation, so Pakistanis did it for them. When Bahamian Buddhas were blown up by the Afghan Taliban, the expertise was provided by Pakistani and Saudi engineers.

Throughout the nineties, when American targets were being attacked in many parts of the world by Al-Qaeda, many, if not most, of its members used the Pakistani port city of Karachi as a transit point to fly in and out of Pakistan and to reach Afghanistan by road. There is every reason to believe that Pakistanis could have easily tracked and stopped them had they wanted to do so. The inconvenient conclusion: whether directly or indirectly, Pakistan was aiding Al-Qaeda. Therefore, it is hardly surprising that, even after its defeat at the hands of America and its allies, the Afghan Taliban—

brainchild of Pakistani intelligence—is now back in force, again emerging from Pakistan.[17]

Even if Gen. Pervez Musharraf, the Pakistani leader, is personally sincere about ending Pakistan's support for the Taliban, the establishment in Pakistan—especially the ISI, a deeply political Islam-influenced institution—obviously has other ideas. In December 2006 a captured Taliban spokesman told Afghan investigators that the Taliban would never have been able to challenge Afghan military and NATO forces without the direct assistance of Pakistan's ISI.[18] This goes to prove that the most influential entity in Pakistan is political Islam.

The writ of Hamid Karzai's government is now mostly restricted to Kabul and its surrounding areas. This does not bode well for the possibility of a democratic or a pro-western regime in Afghanistan in the future. Now Pakistani officials are urging NATO countries to accept the Taliban and to work towards a new coalition government in Kabul that might exclude the Afghan president Hamid Karzai. Pakistan's foreign minister, Khurshid Kasuri, has said in private briefings to foreign ministers of some NATO member states that the Taliban are winning the war in Afghanistan and NATO is bound to fail. He has advised against sending more troops.[19]

Axis of Jihad

We have now come to realize that political Islam and jihad have spread throughout the world due to the ideological and financial sponsorship of many Islamic nations. However, as discussed before, three nations stand out due to their leadership in this unsavory endeavor: Saudi Arabia, Iran and Pakistan—here called the "Axis of Jihad". Of these nations, Iran and Saudi Arabia are regional rivals, as are Iran and Pakistan. Nonetheless, this axis has a common vision—that of conquest of unbelievers and their lands, and the use of terror as a long-standing instrument of this vision. Evidence is put together here to show the axis nations' sponsorship of terror in many parts of the world where Muslims exist in sizable numbers. This has continued even after the 9/11 attacks. Once more, this goes to show that America and its allies need a new policy vis-à-vis the so-called allies: Saudi Arabia and Pakistan.

Why only these three nations? Why not Syria, the United Arab Emirates, Bangladesh or some other Islamic states? The secular Syrian regime uses terrorism as part of its military and foreign policy strategy, but not as a jihad tool. The United Arab Emirates and Bangladesh have been influenced into jihad by Saudi Arabia and Pakistan, respectively. In terms of scale, as well as ideological and physical commitment toward jihad-sponsorship, the axis nations can be seen as the leaders and many other Islamic states—the followers.

Saudi Arabia funds mosques, trains preachers, and builds schools across the globe that teach virulent Wahhabi Islam, which views the outside world and modernity with hatred. This is part of an integral strategy to infect Muslim populations with jihadism and get them to identify with Saudi interests. Jihadism is the necessary instrument for conquest of "infidel" lands; therefore, it is given importance in Saudi society because political Islam is, by far, the domineering force in Saudi Arabia. In other words, jihad is a Saudi Arabian passion. Therefore, this book rejects the widely held notion that Saudi Arabia supports jihad as a way of deflecting and diverting internal jihadist pressure.

Saudi Arabia has allowed private individuals and charities to donate to terrorist causes in Kashmir, Chechnya, Bosnia and Afghanistan. Over two decades, the Saudi royal family has spent about 85-90 billion dollars of its oil wealth to finance some 1350 new mosques, 210 Islamic centers, and hundreds of universities in Europe, the Americas, Asia and Africa.[20] These Saudi-funded organizations have been hotbeds of anti-Western and particularly anti-American indoctrination. The schools, for example, not only indoctrinate students in a virulent and extreme form of Islam, but also teach them to hate secular Western values. They are also taught to view America as the center of "infidel" power in the world and the enemy of Islam.[21] Graduates of these schools are frequent recruits for Bin Laden's Al-Qaeda terror network, as well as other extremist groups.

In a 2001 article in *The Spectator* of London, Stephen Schwartz points out that people who have embraced Wahhabism have conducted every major terrorist attack against the West in recent years. "Bin Laden is a Wahhabi. So are the suicide bombers in Israel. So are his Egyptian allies, who exulted as they stabbed foreign tourists to death at Luxor... So are the Algerian terrorists... So are the Taliban-style guerrillas who murder Hindus in Kashmir... None of this extremism has been inspired by American fumbling in the world, and it has little to do with the tragedies that have beset Israelis and Palestinians."[22]

It is clear that Saudi Arabia now exports two products around the globe—petroleum products and religious fanaticism. In 2005, Saudi Arabia's secretary-general of the official Muslim World League Koran Memorization Commission, Sheikh Abdallah Basfar, urged Muslims everywhere to fund terrorism. He declared, "The Prophet said: 'He who equips a fighter—it is as if he himself fought.' You lie in your bed, safe in your own home, and donate money and Allah credits you with the rewards of a fighter. What is this? A privilege."[23]

The Saudi investment in jihad is paying off. A June 2006 Pew Global Attitudes poll showed that a majority of Muslims in Jordan, Egypt and Nigeria, as well as roughly a third of Muslim residents in France, Spain and Great Britain, felt violence against civilians can be justified in order to defend Islam.[24] Of course, it is left to medieval clerics, who are invariably extremists, to define when and where Islam needs to be defended. Thus from a practical perspective, this poll indicates that a majority of Muslims in many Muslim nations support terror against non-Muslim civilians.

From a *Reader's Digest* article detailing Saudi sponsorship of terror worldwide:

It has been pointed out that Saudi officials have, at minimum, a clear pattern of looking the other way when funds are known to support extremist purposes. Even after 2001, Saudi officials continue to support organizations that finance international terrorism. It has also channeled funds to Hamas and other groups that have committed terrorist acts in Israel and other portions of the Middle East. The Bosnia and

Herzegovina offices of Al-Haramain Islamic Foundation, for example, are accused by the US Treasury Department of funneling money earmarked for orphanages and mosques in Mogadishu, Somalia, to a local terrorist group linked to Al-Qaeda. Al-Haramain is active in more than 50 countries. Officials of the Saudi Arabia-based (International Islamic Relief Organization) IIRO have also been implicated in terrorism around the world, according to testimony to the US Congress from Mr. Levitt, a former FBI agent...

The IIRO' Manila office was headed for eight years by Osama Bin Laden's brother-in-law, Muhammad Jamal Khalifa, "through which he sent funds to terrorist groups affiliated with Al Qaeda, including Abu Sayyaf" said Levitt. "IIRO is part of the Muslim World League, which is funded and supported by the Saudi government." Saudi Arabian officials claim that any involvement of these organizations with terrorism is the work of "rogue elements." But few people believe this claim. "All individuals running overseas charities are government appointed and the government watches every penny," a Saudi academic told Reader's Digest in the country's capital, Riyadh... Much of the money comes directly from the Saudi king himself, Fahd Bin Abdul Aziz Al Saud... In Pakistan, Kashmir, the newly-independent Central Asian republics, and Chechnya, Saudi religious and charitable agencies have encouraged radical Islamists and armed rebellion against secular governments. "It's hard to know where the line is drawn between funding charity and weapons for insurgents or money for terrorists," says Ahmed Rashid, a leading Pakistani expert and author of a best-selling book about the Taliban...

Saudi money has also financed thousands of religious seminaries in Pakistan, Afghanistan, Central Asia and Africa. Professor Vali Nasr, a US-based expert on Islamic extremism, characterizes many of the seminaries as "Islamic West Points mixing a dosage of Islam with a lot of military training...Many members of Bin Laden's Al-Qaeda network are graduates of these Saudi-funded schools... In Western Europe, from Edinburgh to Lisbon, from Brussels to Moscow, a large number of mosques, Islamic centers and schools are now under Saudi control.[20]

Excerpts from Steve Emerson's statement before the 9/11 Commission on Saudi sponsorship of terror:

Nazir Qureshi is assistant Secretary-General of WAMY—a Saudi charity. He has been accused by the Indian government of supplying money to Kashmiri terrorist groups headed by Syed Ali Shah Geelani. The Pakistani paper The News reported on March 25, 2001 that the Pakistani youth organization *Jamiat Taleba Arabia* is the only Pakistan-based member organization of WAMY. The article continued, "WAMY is also involved in religious and *Jehadi* training for its member organizations."...

According to The News, *Jamiat Taleba Arabia*, the WAMY member-organization, was: "involved in

Afghanistan from the very beginning. It joined the *Jehad* in Kashmir as soon as the Kashmiris started their armed struggle in 1990 and was fully involved by 1993. The members of the *Jamiat Taleba Arabia* fought under the umbrella of Gulbadin Hakmatyar's *Hizbe Islami* in Afghanistan and, in Occupied Kashmir, under the discipline of the *hizbul Mujahideen*...Jehad has become the focus of the *Jamiat's* activities in the last two decades..."

According to the Indian magazine *Frontline*, Mohammed Ayyub Thukar, President of the World Kashmir Freedom Movement, was a financier of *Hizbul Mujahideen*, a Kashmiri terror organization. During his exile in Saudi Arabia, Thukar was affiliated with MWL, WAMY, and the Muslim Brotherhood. Sardar Ija Afzal Khan, Amir of *Jamaat-e-Islami* since early June, 2002, "highlighted [the] freedom struggle of the Kashmiris at the forums of World Assembly of Muslim Youth..." The Indian government contends that "90 percent of the funding [for Kashmir militants] is from other countries and Islamic organizations like the World Association of Muslim Youth".[25]

Only after the May and November 2003 attacks in the mainland did the Saudis crackdown on homegrown extremists. Nonetheless, unofficial Saudi financial support for the radical Wahhabi movement continues. One new Saudi document found in Palestinian offices demonstrated that the Saudis were aiding Palestinian families involved in suicide attacks on Israel.[15]

"Funds are available for the asking for *LeT* (*Lashkar-e-Taiba*, an India-specific terror outfit based in Pakistan) not only from Pakistan, but also from Wahhabi fundamentalists in Saudi Arabia and the UAE," says an ex-activist of Student Islamic Movement of India (SIMI)—a potential evidence of jihad directed at non-Muslim Indians.[26]

A report on terrorism in South East Asia notes Saudi Arabia and Pakistan working together to fund jihad:

In recent years, said Rohan Gunaratna, who heads a Singaporean research center on terror, Saudi Arabia has financed much of the terror in Southeast Asia. Until 2003, funds went from the Saudis, supposedly U.S. allies, to al Qaeda and through Pakistan to Southeast Asia. After the Pakistan channel was disrupted, funds have been sent directly from Saudi Arabia...

Mr. Gunaratna said terrorists in Southeast Asia are increasingly driven by ideology, which calls for setting up an Islamic state centered on Indonesia, the world's most populous Muslim nation. It would include the southern Philippines, Malaysia, and southern Thailand, which have large Muslim populations. "Asian groups," he said, "are becoming Arabized." [27]

According to the Indian scholar R. Upadhyay, funding for terrorism sponsorship in Bangladesh is originating from the Middle East:

Direct funding to the terrorist outfits in Bangladesh from international NGOs like Kuwait-based Revival of

Islamic Heritage, Saudi Arabia-based Al Haramaine Islamic Institute, Rabita Al Alam Al Islami, Qatar Charitable Society... [were] primarily responsible for fomenting extremism, training and recruiting of youths to carry out jihadi activities.[28]

Iran's sponsorship of jihad is not as extensive as Saudi Arabia's; it is mostly specific to Shiite communities. Hizbollah received tactical guidance from Iranian diplomats, fundamentalist ideology from Iranian clerics and training in Iran. A state subsidy of about $100 million was also given to Hizbollah in the 1980s for "humanitarian and social work."[29]

In 1992, terrorists who were suspected of being sponsored by Iran bombed a synagogue in Argentina. Finally, in 1998, a telephone call intercepted from the Iranian embassy in Argentina demonstrated Iran's involvement. Argentina immediately expelled six of the seven Iranian diplomats in the country.[29] Even today, this bombing remains unsolved.

Israel's 2006 thrust into Lebanon to retrieve its captured soldiers by Hizbollah was met with fierce rocket attacks, indiscriminately aimed at civilian areas in Israel. Many of these rockets were said to have been given to Hizbollah by Iran.[30]

According to Daniel Byman, Pakistan is funding, arming, training and providing diplomatic support for varied terrorist groups that are active in Indian Kashmir. So close is the tie between the Pakistani state and these outfits that Pakistani intelligence unit, ISI, "selects targets, including civilian ones, and knows about major attacks in advance".[31] Pakistan also inserted foreign fighters from Taliban and Al-

Qaeda into India.[32] A Pakistan-based jihad commander named Syed Salahuddin said in a 2006 interview, "We can hit any soft target anywhere in India".[33]

Showing the focus of Pakistan's India-directed jihad is a 2005 study by Rubina Saigol, Country Director, Action Aid, Pakistan:

> About 8,000 Pakistani Punjabis, about 3,000 from the North-West Frontier Province and about 500 from Sindh are estimated to have died as jihadists in Indian Kashmir since 1989. In comparison, only 112 Balochs have died as jihadists, mostly in Afghanistan.[34]

At a 2006 conference on terrorism in Bombay, a number of non-Muslim activists from Islamic Bangladesh spoke. Alleging Islamic militant organizations' involvement in a large number of rapes and murders in the region, Prajnalankar Bhikku, an activist from Bangladesh, said: "A silent genocide and ethnic cleansing (of non-Muslims) is taking place in the hills of Bangladesh without the knowledge of the outside world." Journalist and activist Shahriar Kabir cites the rise of militant organizations as the reason. "On the one hand, the West asks [Pakistan President] General [Pervez] Musharraf to take action against fundamentalists in that country. On the other, it supports the four-party fundamentalist coalition in Bangladesh. The United States and other nations must ask Pakistan and Saudi Arabia to stop funding these fundamentalist organizations,".[35]

Pakistan's track record of butchering and terrorizing the non-Muslim population is well recorded. In 1971 it launched a military strike in what was then East Pakistan (now known as Bangladesh) by selectively choosing non-Muslims to murder or to expel to India, in order to cleanse the region of "infidels".

From Pakistan's own Hommadur Rahman Commission report on 1971 war:

> There was a general feeling of hatred against Bengalis amongst the soldiers and officers, including Generals. There were verbal instructions to eliminate Hindus. The statements appearing in the evidence of Lt. Col. Aziz Ahmed Khan (Witness no 276) who was Commanding Officer 8 Baluch and then CO 86 Mujahid Battalion are also directly relevant. "Brigadier Arbbab also told me to destroy all houses in Joydepur. To a great extent I executed this order. General Niazi visited my unit at Thakurgaon and Bogra. He asked us how many Hindus we had killed. In May, there was an order in writing to kill Hindus. This order was from Brigadier Abdullah Malik of 23 Brigade."[36]

Before the Indian Army finally subdued Pakistani army and its local collaborators, they had slaughtered up to 3 million Bengalis in nine months of unabated killings throughout the summer of 1971.[37]

The Pakistani army moved methodically from village to village, leaving a trail of destruction in its wake. Sydney Schanberg of the *New York Times* described the systematic subjugation and killing of Bengalis:

Army trucks roll through the half-deserted streets of the capital of East Pakistan these days, carrying "antistate" prisoners to work-sites for hard labor. Their heads are shaved and they wear no shoes and no clothes except for shorts—all making escape difficult. Street designations are being changed to remove all Hindu names as well as those of Bengali Moslem nationalists as part of a campaign to stamp out Bengali culture. Shankari Bazar Road in Dacca is now Tikka Khan Road, after the lieutenant general governor of East Pakistan, whom most Bengalis call "the Butcher."

Since the offensive began the troops have killed countless thousands of Bengalis—foreign diplomats estimate at least 200,000 to 250,000—many in massacres. Although the targets were Bengali Moslems and the 10 million Hindus at first, the army is now concentrating on Hindus in what foreign observers characterize as a holy war... 'Of the more than six million Bengalis who are believed to have fled to India to escape the army's terror, at least four million are Hindus. The troops are still killing Hindus and burning and looting their villages.[37]

As Pakistan was never held accountable for these crimes against humanity, it was predictably emboldened to do more of the same in the coming decades. Indeed, this was to repeat again in the 1980s, '90s and in this century (more details in Chapter Three).

Several pointers from this data and analysis: axis-of-jihad nations are the prime movers and shakers behind radical Islamic terrorism and the resulting war on terror. These nations have learned little from the 9/11 attacks on America. This is because they have not been held accountable. American efforts to engage "moderate" rulers of these nations are a failure, because this has not stopped jihad from emanating from these nations. Unfortunately, hostile relations have limited American influence over Iran.

There is no doubt that, at least at a limited level, American policymakers and lawmakers have been aware of Saudi Arabian or Pakistani roles in sponsoring worldwide jihad. Dependence on oil and Pakistan's status as a nuclear power have limited American options, as has America's limited understanding of the enemy ideology. Alternate ideas on dealing with these nations are taken up in the last chapter, which addresses policy response.

The "democracy approach" to neutralizing political Islam was taken soon after the 9/11 attacks.[38] Regrettably, the project to democratize Iraq has diverted attention from axis of jihad. Although American efforts in Iraq now stand discredited, there are many in legislative and executive branches and in the American bureaucracy who still think of democracy as the antidote to terror. The coming section discusses why this democracy hypothesis is flawed and points out what factors lead to functional democracies and terror disengagement.

The Democracy Angle

In response to the 9/11 attacks on America, some neoconservatives close to centers of power in Washington

39

had felt that if a successful democracy could be introduced at the heart of the Middle East, then perhaps democracy would retard growth of radical Islam in the host nation. It was thought that this success would encourage the flowering of democracy in nearby nations and eventually triumph over radical Islam. Iraq seemed to be a good candidate, with the secular dictatorship of Saddam Hussein already keeping radical Islam at bay. Iraq also had a fairly well-educated population, and importantly, Al-Qaeda didn't seem to have any following there. With the world's second largest oil deposits in Iraq, financing this democracy project appeared feasible. Iraq was already under a UN-sponsored sanctions regime, and any apparent violation subjected it to external intervention. Also among the lessons America learned from 9/11 attacks was the need for preemption (which was to be applied later in the case of Iraq intervention): never allow an enemy with a track record of violence directed at American interests to develop the ability to launch strikes.

When the Bush administration claimed to be in possession of data indicating development of weapons of mass destruction in Hussein's Iraq—in violation of the sanctions regime, and potentially threatening the national security of the United States—the die was cast and an opportunity presented itself for an invasion. If this data is indeed true, there may be some justification for invading and removing Hussein on the grounds of preemption. However, there is much controversy now as to whether this data is genuine or was cooked up to justify the intervention. This may be one of the issues the current Democrat-controlled Congress will look into.

After the swift removal of Saddam's Baathist regime, despite the ongoing American occupation, the democracy project is clearly failing in Iraq. It now appears, as analyzed in a Bob Woodward's book, that there was really no plan to build a functional democracy in Iraq after takeover.[38] Clearly, meddling by Iraq's neighbors has not helped the allied effort. The Bush administration officials seem to have thought that once the Baathist regime was taken out of power, everything else would fall into place.

"Nation-building" refers to the process of constructing or structuring a nation with the aid of armed forces. The armed forces in such a situation are used with the aim of unifying people or peoples within the state and to of making the situation politically stable and viable in the long run. Nation-building also involves the use of propaganda or major infrastructure development to foster social harmony and economic growth. Nation-building helps empower the populace to practice democracy and help build institutions for governance. But the Bush administration appears not to have thought through two critical questions: whether the Iraqi Muslim majority population—although no ally of Al-Qaeda—would embrace a largely Christian and white occupying force, and whether this population had desire for nation-building. A lack of affinity for jihad, even a desire to participate in free polls, doesn't necessarily translate into the desire for nation-building. This is an observation that was made painfully obvious by the failed American effort to establish a robust democracy in Haiti.[39]

It is useful to discuss under what conditions American efforts at nation-building had succeeded in the past. In the immediate aftermath of World War II, along with allies, the

United States stationed its army in both Germany and Japan. The US then helped to rewrite their constitutions, brought stability, and helped build these devastated nations into leading economies. In the case of Germany, Nazi ideology stood comprehensively defeated and its former rulers were vanquished. Emperor Hirohito of Japan ordered surrender to the Americans and told his people to cooperate. With the imperial army adjusting to the emperor's wishes, there was hardly any sustained insurgency by the locals. In the end, the American occupation was a win-win for all parties. What also helped is that the citizens of these countries had an outlook similar to that of America; they had the desire and know-how for nation-building, even before the war.

American efforts at nation-building had also succeeded in South Korea, which unlike Germany and Japan had no prior experience or ability in nation-building. South Korea, which was economically comparable to India in the 1950s, latched on to the opportunity provided by America to become a high-power economy. Here the South Koreans had the right "outlook"—that of willing to learn and follow America and not mount insurgencies. One could argue that, threatened by Communist North Korea and China, South Koreans had limited options. In all of these cases, Germany, Japan or Korea there existed no ideology or institutions with a strong grass-roots base that was opposed to American involvement.

Democracy and Islam

The situation in Afghanistan and Iraq was different. After swift military victories in Iraq and in Afghanistan, not knowing any better, American policy makers allowed political Islam to fill the power vacuum.

Thinking they were doing a good deed, Americans gave spiritual "access" to the Iraqi public that they had liberated from Saddam's oppressive, yet secular Baathist regime. This was not a smart move, as political Islam in Iraq is ideologically opposed to a western-styled democracy. This shouldn't be a surprise; as we will see later, political Islam as practiced in most Muslim nations believes in jihad-building, not nation-building; Muslim religious institutions form nodes of social networks among Muslim communities and are well-positioned to spawn insurgencies. By allowing mosques and clerics to enter the center stage, America may inadvertently have laid the foundation for a no-win situation.

In Afghanistan, America was more careful. But years of Saudi funding and Pakistani involvement had helped install hard-line clerics in its many mosques. Subsequent to the American invasion, after the initial restraint, many clergy, especially among the Pashtun majority, have turned up the anti-American rhetoric. This has undermined the allied effort to build reliable local security forces and the whole effort of nation-building there. The other major problem is a resurgent Taliban infiltration from Pakistan—also home to a Pashtun population.

The ways in which political Islam is undermining America and its allies' good-faith effort in both Iraq and Afghanistan are explained in an analysis by Edward Luttwak:

Since the 2003 invasion, both Shiite and Sunni clerics have been repeating over and over again that the Americans and their "Christian" allies have come to

Iraq to destroy Islam in its cultural heartland and to steal the country's oil. The clerics dismiss all talk of democracy and human rights by the invaders as mere hypocrisy—with the exception of women's rights, which the clerics say are only propagandized to persuade Iraqi daughters and wives to dishonor their families by imitating the shameless nakedness and impertinence of Western women.

The vast majority of Afghans and Iraqis naturally believe their religious leaders. The alternative would be to believe what for them is entirely unbelievable: that foreigners are unselfishly expending blood and treasure in order to help them. They themselves would never invade a foreign country except to plunder it, the way Iraq invaded Kuwait, thus having made Saddam Hussein genuinely popular for a time when troops brought back their loot. As many opinion polls and countless incidents demonstrate, the Americans and their allies are widely considered to be the worst of invaders, who came to rob Muslim Iraqis not only of their territory and oil but also of their religion and even their family honor. Many Muslims around the world believe as much, even in Turkey, whose most successful recent film depicted an American Jewish military doctor who was operating on Iraqis not to save their lives but to remove their kidneys, which of course he was sending back to the U.S. for transplantation and his personal profit (he was Jewish after all). It is the same in Afghanistan, where the American-imposed quota of women parliamentarians has caused widespread resentment, not least because most Afghans are scandalized by the spectacle of a woman contradicting a man in public— as in, for example, televised parliamentary debates.[40]

In this new war some costly mistakes are going to made; the Iraq occupation may be one of them.[41] The issue of whether it is possible to bring functional democracy to Islamic nations with a history of repression and dominance of political Islam is worthy of study. Below is a letter written by the author that was published in the *Washington Times*:

Pakistan's undemocratic underpinnings

The conclusions found in "Studies say elites spurred to terror" (Business, Wednesday) are incomplete. The question should be what causes political repression?

Pakistan and India were created in 1947 in British-ruled India. When the British left, both of these nations inherited democracy. Hindu-majority India has remained secular and democratic, but Muslim-majority Pakistan couldn't sustain democracy and is now a dictatorship. Pakistan also has become a dominant source and sponsor of Islamic terrorism.

Pakistan couldn't sustain democracy because the retrogressive political indoctrination taught in its mosques does not allow the separation of church and state. This has led to political repression amid a flowering of Islamic fundamentalism.

This conclusion tells us that if the United States wants to make any Islamic state a model nation for democracy, it must first address the issue of the hateful and retrogressive preaching in its mosques.[42]

The author explores these ideas further in another letter published in the *Washington Times* (excerpts):

A new paradigm for the war on terror

I am writing to request that the Bush administration revisit the idea of pulling troops out of Iraq, where the general tide is going against America. I would like to give an alternate view to William Taylor's column ("War and impatience," Commentary, Saturday).

The virtual absence of democracy in the Islamic world points to fundamental flaws in Islam that must first be fixed before democracy can take root. Political and retrogressive preaching by most Muslim clerics does not allow for the separation of mosque and state, and leads to repressive regimes such as Saddam Hussein's in Iraq. America is already a target of these clerics in Iraq, who are doing everything to undermine America's desire to bring democracy there.

A pullback now from Iraq will probably lead to a takeover by another repressive regime hostile to American interests. But such a regime inherits an Iraq with weakened infrastructure—and a much less developed ability to create weapons of destruction. However, it is much better than the no-win situation America now finds itself in Iraq.[43]

Apart from religion, India and Pakistan share history, language, food habits, and culture. Hence, the difference in outlook should have been shaped by the respective majority religions. It should be noted that the outlook of Pakistan had been predisposed toward radicalism well before the 1970s infusion of petrodollars. The next chapter will discuss the reasons for this outlook in greater detail.

Since Muslim religious institutions work at the grass-roots level, with resources and in a democratic environment, they are best placed to bring about jihadization of Muslim communities. We are seeing this occurring in just about all Muslim communities around the world, even under democracy. This is a bad news for those who claim that democracy is an antidote to radical Islam! In the last chapter on policy response, some ideas are presented on how political Islam can be repelled within a democratic setup.

The power and influence attained by mosques, due to their political inclinations, is well-known. As discussed in the author's letter listed in previous pages, political preaching and its retrogressive nature disrupt the functioning of a state. This must be seen as the hallmark of political Islam in the modern times. This has made even non-Islamist regimes in the Middle East unable to make progress, in terms of development and in the process of democratization. This is true in Egypt and in Saddam's Iraq, where the state in many ways regulated what was said in influential mosques. Yet clerical sermons, whether directly or indirectly have undermined authority and nation-building. Also, retrogressive sermons discourage modern education, which is a must for wealth creation and progress. This eventually creates conditions of dissatisfaction and impoverishment, setting the stage for Islamic radicals, pushed to the front by political Islam, to gain power through ballot box.

Like the radical Muslim Brotherhood in Egypt, its offshoot in the West Bank, Hamas, has understood the importance of providing social services. Before coming to power, this radical group had managed to come across as caring and as a "defender" of the people, through suicide attacks directed at Israel, in sharp contrast to the dysfunctional Palestinian authority. This shows how political Islamic organizations can use the ballot box and "service" to reach power. Once such a politico-religious organization comes to power, the business becomes exporting jihad externally and consolidating the internal process of Islamization through repression.

Not surprisingly, in representing political Islam, organizations such as Hamas have no vision for development. Iran is another example of a country in which Islamist gained power through the ballot box and then pursued jihad-spreading policies. Once radicals get set in power it is hard to get rid of them through internal mechanisms, due to their control of the military and the mosque, the two strong institutions which would be capable of challenging them. In all likelihood, such a nation, whether or not it is democratic, will become a fountainhead for jihad.

What is more interesting is the dynamics of Islam within India itself, a secular democratic nation where Muslims are a minority. Contrary to general perception, all the available evidence indicates political Islam's dominance of the Indian Muslim community. At the moment, India is reeling under an escalating surge of home-grown Islamic terrorism. Because Indian democracy is effectively under siege by Islamist radicals, India finds itself unable to undertake decisive steps to deal with this threat (this will be discussed further in the third chapter). A successful siege of India by political Islam may be discounted if India is viewed as a largely dysfunctional democracy.

However, home-grown Islamic terrorism in England has shown how political Islam can recruit activists even in a developed multi-ethnic functional democracy. Clearly, it has taken radical Islamic elements decades to indoctrinate young Muslims, typically of Pakistani ethnicity. In the name of religious freedom, clerics were imported from Pakistan or from Middle Eastern nations. Knowing little English and reared in repressive Islamic countries with a strong political Islamic base, most of these clerics had one qualification— their ability to indoctrinate impressionable young minds towards jihad.

Several important conclusions can be derived from the above sections. Muslim populations can be radicalized under varying conditions; in Muslim majority countries with a strong political Islamic presence, it is hard to establish functional democracies; ballot-box opportunity will likely be taken advantage of by radicals, who take the opportunity to gain power in order to sponsor jihad through the state apparatus.

Democracy Through Wealth Creation

Given the ongoing debacle in Iraq, many would consider security, rather than democracy-building, to be the primary objective of the United States vis-à-vis war on terror.

But as we will see in this section, the ingredients that are incorporated in making functional democracies also tend to lead to nations that focus on nation-building and trade. In short, such nations' primary or secondary passion would not be conquest of unbelievers.

How can functional democracies be built? It is argued here that providing the conditions to create wealth will eventually lead to developing functional democracies.

Wealth creation is about manufacturing technically sophisticated products that can be used for trade and for internal consumption. This is what distinguishes "developed" nations from "developing" nations. For the manufacturer, the ability to trade generates wealth, which is the most important requirement for survival. Wealth creation also requires an entrepreneur-oriented capitalistic system that allows healthy competition, a system of laws protecting property rights, a world-class education system, and rigorous enforcement of law and order.

A church that is heavily mixing politics with religion is interfering with governance. Hence, separation of church and state is necessary to enact and enforce laws that are appropriate for the contemporary world.

Wealth creation is a win-win situation, producing not just wealth itself, but also a capable population. Wealth creation can also be seen as the intended consequence of nation-building, the necessary process before achieving a functional democracy.

To create wealth, people have to learn to work together—the very same requirement needed to make a democracy functional. As well, the required conditions for creating wealth indirectly undermine corruption, which is a common and debilitating problem in developing nations practicing democracy. Once the fruits of wealth creation begin to reach the masses, they too embrace the philosophy of wealth creation, rather than manipulating the system through corrupt practices designed to garner wealth for themselves and their families.

During the last fifty years, many formerly developing nations have achieved prosperity and, eventually, functional democracies on the basis of wealth creation and stability, achieved through non-democratic modes of governing. The East Asian nations of Taiwan, Singapore, and South Korea, have shown that economic growth can be achieved through policies encouraging wealth creation, although some rights are sacrificed in the short-term. This can lead to long-term dividends of economic prosperity, stability, and, importantly, a natural transition to functional democracy. The non-democratic mode of governing ensures stability and order during the transition period. Also notable in these nations is the near absence of strong institutions with retrogressive and ideological agendas.

Without stability, a regime's energy, time and scarce resources may be wasted. This is the case with India. Although the Indian economy is growing, as we will see in chapter three, escalating instabilities are threatening to unravel a largely nonfunctioning Indian democracy.

In the past fifty years, there is almost no example of a nation graduating from a developing to a developed country through democracy. It is not hard to see why. When a country is developing, its citizens generally have yet to develop skills to work together to solve problems. When such a people are given a voice, governing becomes almost impossible. The lack of problem-solving skills is reflected in the leadership. The press and media also become very vocal and tend not to be particularly constructive, lacking vision and abilities, as is so common among their colleagues in developed countries.

The African nation of Malawi has had free elections, a multi-party system, and a free press since 1994, and can arguably call itself a democracy. Yet democracy in Malawi is now considered to be a failure due to poor governance.[44] Democracy is clearly failing in Africa's largest nation, Nigeria, and in several more African nations—in Gambia, Uganda, Ethiopia and Zambia.[45] American efforts to bring democracy to Haiti after the departure of "Baby Doc" has also been considered a failure in many ways.[39]

In developing democracies, a destabilizing force can arise in the form of insurgencies mounted by minorities (as is the case in India—discussed in Chapter Three) or by a strong institution that does not believe in the separation of religion and state and that is jihad-building in its outlook (e.g., political Islam in Pakistan). These instabilities often become too hot to handle, as elected politicians, being answerable to the public, cannot afford to be seen to be ruthless in dealing with these problems. Many of these democracies never end up resolving these problems, which often have devastating consequences as a result.

But nations ruled by undemocratic regimes often can deal with destabilizing forces ruthlessly and effectively, as the regime's leaders are not answerable to the public. Chinese leaders have understood the importance of stability in economic development and wealth creation.[46] The student movement in the early nineties for democracy was ruthlessly crushed. Among the reasons given by the Chinese leadership was the instability that the ongoing movement would bring. Investments in China really took off after that. Western leaders, who overwhelmingly supported this nascent democracy movement, probably never took home the lesson: the importance of stability in nations embarking on wealth creation.

Even democratic nations, faced with certain forms of destabilization, find themselves using undemocratic means, such as massively violating human rights in order to be effective. This was true of American approach to dealing with native Americans.

Fareed Zakaria, in a live talk, stated: "Dictatorships are great for economic growth when they have the right ideas and implement them well. China has grown faster than any country in the world for this reason. Trouble is, how do you make sure you get a dictator like Lee Kuan Yew and not Mobutu (Seko) or (Ferdinand) Marcos?".[47]

One strong man or a woman cannot dictate a system unless the system is receptive to them. Make no mistake! Kuan Yew's visionary leadership was critical for Singapore. However, he still had to rely on a system to get the job done. Kuan Yew would be hard pressed to repeat his miracle in Zaire, where Mobutu ruled. Looking at it in a different way, if Zaire ends up having a dictator, in all likelihood it will be someone like Mobutu, a thug who is only interested in lining his and his cronies' pockets.

A nation's leader typically reflects the nation. If a nation decides against the suitability of democratic mode of governing with regard to warding off instabilities, and goes for an authoritarian rule, the system in the country, defined by culture, outlook, and religion, will likely determine the nature of the authoritarian rule. It doesn't happen randomly, as Zakaria implies.

We may arrive at an important conclusion: Wealth creation, rather than democracy, is the basis for building modern civilizations. A well-developed and functional democracy is the eventual consequence of such a wealth creation process.

There is another bonus: an educated and informed population, shaped by wealth creation, is not going to be brainwashed by medieval and retrogressive religious priests. One can now understand why it is not in the best interests of political Islam to create conditions for generating wealth. We have already seen—in Iraq, Afghanistan, Pakistan, and even in Palestinian territories—that trying to create a functional democracy, without neutralizing political Islam, is a ticket to nowhere. Yet the establishment in Washington, in a bipartisan way, continues to preach the establishment of democracy in Muslim world—without neutralizing political Islam—as the answer to winning war on terror.

Where does this hypothesis, that wealth creation is the necessary precursor to a functional democracy, put nations endowed with natural wealth? The reality is that exceptional levels of inherited wealth at the individual level or the societal level discourages further wealth creation in a developing nation. When combined with entrenched, expansionist and retrogressive ideologies such as political Islam, this can lead to terror sponsorship as a channel for using the new-found wealth.

Yet inherited wealth is a one-trick pony. It does not ensure wealth for most, nor it is likely to be sustaining. Most Saudis and Iranians know this only too well, when high population growth rates and falling oil prices led to a significant drop in per capita income. The Saudi Arabian oil economy can provide only one job per three young men coming into the work force.[48] Although Iran has increased its oil production over the years, increased consumption has led to a net decrease in oil exports. Some of its big and old oil wells are also showing signs of decline. For a nation deriving about 85 percent of its export income from oil sales, these are not good signs.[49]

9/11 Commission's Recommendations

The Commission was an independent and bipartisan entity, created by congressional legislation and receiving the signature of President George W. Bush in late 2002. It was chartered to prepare a full and complete account of the circumstances surrounding the September 11, 2001 terrorist attacks, including our preparedness for and immediate response to the attacks. The Commission was also mandated to provide recommendations designed to guard against future attacks.

The Commission has made several valuable suggestions on how a coalition, especially one comprising non-Muslim states, can be put together against what it calls "radical Islam". It also overviews funding for terrorism and provides good ideas on curtailing financial support for terror organizations.

But the Commission, in views of many, has underestimated the strength of radical Islam, calling it a "minority tradition" and has downplayed the importance of jihad as a tool for political Islamic conquest. Andrew Bostom made an admirable but futile appeal to the Commission: "Although time grows dangerously short, it is not too late for the 9/11 Commissioners and, more importantly, those who share their assessment to broaden their understanding of the depth of the ideological threat posed by jihad ".[50]

How can the United States and its friends help moderate Muslims to combat extremist ideas? Here is the 9/11 Commission's recommendation:

> The U.S. government must define what the message is, what it stands for. We should offer an example of moral leadership in the world, committed to treat people humanely, abide by the rule of law, and be generous and caring to our neighbors. America and Muslim friends can agree on respect for human dignity and opportunity. To Muslim parents, terrorists like Bin Laden have nothing to offer their children but visions of violence and death. America and its friends have a crucial advantage—we can offer these parents a vision that might give their children a better future. If we heed the views of thoughtful leaders in the Arab and Muslim world, a moderate consensus can be found.[51]

As pointed out in subsequent chapters, extremism—not moderation—is the mainstream among Islamic traditions. This distinction means a great deal in terms of outlining effective strategies. For instance, the Commission observes that "cures" or reform must come from within Muslim societies themselves. The United States must support such developments.[51] This book contends that when extremism is mainstream, moderates are simply not empowered enough to reform Islamic society from within; hence, outsiders must step in. Some ideas on accomplishing this are discussed in the chapter on policy response.

The misdiagnosis by the Commission, which is not realizing that extremism among Muslims in certain nations is mainstream, means several of the grand strategies outlined in its report—in particular, the idea of constructive engagement with Pakistan or Saudi Arabia—are limited in scope. The deterioration in both Afghanistan and Iraq and the adverse meddling by its neighbors point to two inevitable realities: 1) These societies do not have a progressive streak worth nurturing, and 2) Muslim states neighboring Afghanistan or Iraq have no interest in seeing these states becoming progressive democratic societies. Hence, coalition-building between America and Muslim states, as suggested by the Commission, will not really be a viable option for some time to come.

The 9/11 Commission's report reflects the then-American establishment's limited understanding of the new enemy, political Islam; its recommendations should be treated accordingly.

Regardless of who rules nations such as Saudi Arabia or Pakistan, the national pastime remains jihad. Indeed, jihadis and other Muslim radicals have consistently claimed that their vision of unbeliever conquest is derived from theology. The next chapter deals with what the unbelievers of the world can learn about the theology or ideology behind political Islam.

Chapter Two

Passion for Conquest

In the aftermath of 9/11, questions were raised whether the September 11, 2001 attacks were in response to American policies in the Middle East. Specifically, America's siding with Israel in the ongoing Israel-Arab conflict and the perceived American economic and cultural domination of Arabs have been cited as factors that came into play. Now a growing number of analysts have come to the conclusion that America had to be attacked, as it is seen as the bulwark against the spread of Islam or Muslim conquest of "infidels". Bernard Lewis notes:

America is now perceived as the leader of what is variously designated as the West, Christendom, or more generally the 'Lands of the Unbelievers.' In this sense the American president is the successor of a long line of rulers—the Byzantine emperors of Constantinople, the Holy Roman emperors in Vienna,

Queen Victoria and her imperial colleagues and successors in Europe. Today as in the past, this world of Christian unbelievers is seen as the only serious force rivaling and obstructing the divinely ordained spread of Islam, resisting and delaying but not preventing its final, inevitable, universal triumph.[52]

As well, the American mode of governing, its separation of church and state, and its democracy are seen as antithetical to the jihadist outlook of a regime, in which people are "subservient" to Allah and follow precisely the extremist interpretation of what is discussed in the Islamic trilogy.[53]

The jihadist desire and action for conquest can't be accommodated with our own desire to live in peace. This chapter, after shortly discussing the evolution of political Islam, articulates some ideas on how its theological underpinnings could be discredited. Undercutting theology is one important way of weakening the nodes—the mosques and madarasas—of the social network that spawns jihad.

Conquest by Design

If an individual wants to capture, control, and rule a land and its people, it is hard to think of a better way than to declare oneself so close to the almighty God as to be the sole purveyor of His "revelations". This gives the leader enormous legitimacy in eyes of the followers. There is another added advantage to mixing religion with the desire for conquest: the fight for conquest can be enduring, the cause taken over by communities and nations long after the founder is gone. If conquest is the primary purpose of the individual, these revelations and the story of his life would betray the intent.[54] Indeed, the words of Allah are only about 17 percent of the Islamic trilogy, but words and actions of Mohammed comprise 83 percent of the trilogy.[55]

An important statistic that betrays the underlying theme of conquest or political intent while giving lip service to spirituality comes in the form of glorifying the founder of Islam. The following quotation is from William Warner, perhaps the first to identify political Islam as the real enemy of unbelievers and to do a statistical analysis of the Islamic trilogy:

> But the Trilogy is clear about the doctrine. At least 75% of Sira (life of Mohammed) is about jihad. About 67% of the Koran written in Mecca is about the unbelievers, or politics. Of the Koran of Medina, 51% is devoted to the unbelievers. About 20% of Bukhari's Hadith is about jihad and politics. Religion is the smallest part of Islamic foundational texts. There are 146 references to Hell in the Koran. Only 6% of those in Hell are there for moral failings—murder, theft, etc. The other 94% of the reasons for being in Hell are for the intellectual sin of disagreeing with Mohammed, a political crime.[5]

The conclusion is clear: for all practical purposes political Islam is *almost* Islam.

Clearly, America needs to understand the religious motives and the vision of jihadis. This "vision" should be derived from the trilogy of Muslim holy books, as these books in the eyes of jihadis represent the only complete knowledge people need. As the original Islamic literature is in Arabic and is not particularly transparent, it is difficult for unbelievers to comprehend. Fortunately, in recent years, at least one scholar has managed the difficult job of translating Islam's trilogy.[5]

Of the three, the Koran is the oldest and is considered to consist of revelations God sent through Islam's founder, Mohammed. The Muslim legal code, *sharia*, is in the Koran. Hadith is a collection of the sayings and actions of Mohammed. Sira is the biography of Mohammed by Ibn Ishaq. The Islamic trilogy is described by jihadis as a manual for humans, just like a manual for a machine.[6]

Mohammed first preached in Mecca for thirteen years. The portion of the Koran revealed in Mecca is called the Meccan Koran. During this period, Mohammed had only a few followers and had to live peacefully among the predominantly non-Muslim Meccans. Accordingly, the Meccan Koran is peaceful, although it considers non-Muslims inferior. An example of the Meccan Koran (73:10):

Listen to what they [unbelievers] say with patience, and leave them with dignity.[5]

Following the death of his protector uncle, Mohammed was run out of town by wealthy Meccans who did not appreciate his sermons. Mohammed took refuge in a nearby town called Medina. This is where Mohamed started building an army on his own, obtained a huge following and military power. This was achieved by sending his followers, as many say, to rob caravans from Mecca, thereby obtaining wealth for himself and his followers.[54] An example of the Medina Koran (8:12):

> Then your Lord spoke to His angels and said, "I will be with you. Give strength to the believers. I will send terror into the unbelievers' hearts, cut off their heads and even the tips of their fingers!"[5]

These two Koranic verses, the earlier one from Mecca and the later one from Medina, appear to contradict each other. The Medina Koran commands violent conquest of unbelievers. According to the Koran, the later verse replaces the earlier verse.[5] That is, whenever there is a contradiction, the Koran of Medina abrogates the Koran of Mecca. Yet these Mecca Koran verses couldn't be done away with completely, as they are considered "God's revelations".

William Warner calls this contradiction symptomatic of the inherent duality of political Islam and points out: "Both sides of the contradiction are true in dualistic logic."[5] He then goes on to discuss situations in nature where duality holds true, such as in quantum mechanics. Unfortunately, this analogy may be taken by Islamists as a scientific justification for political Islam's glaring and hard-to-justify contradictions!

This book takes a simple alternate view. In an ideology designed by an earthly power intent on conquest, depending upon the situation encountered, the ideology should adjust its tactics towards its adversaries in order to survive and to eventually succeed in its quest for conquest. Hence, inconsistencies in the treatment of adversaries are a hallmark of a man-made ideology of conquest. All of this contrasts with a religion that believes in coexistence—which allows its flock to evolve and be respectful of other denominations.

The political foundation of Islam, especially jihad, had a profound impact in the later years. Mary Habeck observes:

> The ideas supported by the jihadis didn't spring from a void, nor are all of them the marginal opinion of a few fanatics. The principle dogmas they assert—that Islam is the one true faith that will dominate the world; that Muslim rulers need to govern by *sharia* alone; that the Koran and Hadith contain the whole truth for determining the righteous life; that there is no separation between religion and the rest of life; and that Muslims are in a state of conflict with the unbelievers—have roots in discussions about Islamic law and theology that began soon after the death of Mohammed and that are supported by important segments of the clergy (ulema) today.[56]

Bassam Tibi, one of the well-respected contemporary Muslim scholars of jihad, had this to say in 1996 about jihad within the context of Islamic theology—noted by Andrew Bostom:

> At its core, Islam is a religious mission to all humanity. Muslims are religiously obliged to disseminate the Islamic faith throughout the world. "We have sent you forth to all mankind" (Q. 34:28). If non-Muslims submit to conversion or subjugation, this call can be pursued peacefully. If they do not, Muslims are obliged to wage war against them. In Islam, peace

requires that non-Muslims submit to the call of Islam, either by converting or by accepting the status of a religious minority and paying the imposed poll tax, *jizya*. World peace, the final stage of the da'wa, is reached only with the conversion or submission of all mankind to Islam...Muslims believe that expansion through war is not aggression but a fulfillment of the Koranic command to spread Islam as a way to peace. The resort to force to disseminate Islam is not war (*harb*), a word that is used only to describe the use of force by non-Muslims. Islamic wars are not *hurub* (the plural of *harb*) but rather *futuhat*, acts of "opening" the world to Islam and expressing Islamic *jihad*. Relations between *dar al-Islam*, the home of peace, and *dar al-harb*, the world of unbelievers, nevertheless take place in a state of war, according to the Koran and to the authoritative commentaries of Islamic jurists. Unbelievers who stand in the way, creating obstacles for the *da'wa*, are blamed for this state of war, for the *da'wa* can be pursued peacefully if others submit to it. In other words, those who resist Islam cause wars and are responsible for them. Only when Muslim power is weak is "temporary truce" allowed (Islamic jurists differ on the definition of "temporary").[57]

Political Islam's demand of following just the trilogy alone, when the trilogy deals only with Arabic way of life as it was over one thousand years ago, can be interpreted as an attempt to impose a tribal Arabic way of life on non-Arabs. Hence it is legitimate and probably correct to see political

Islam as a tool for conquest during the time of Mohammed, and for his extended tribe of Arabs, beyond his time. It can thus be seen as an alien ideology whose purpose is to bring the world population under Arab control. Hence one may view jihadis as the contemporary activists of the old conquest.

The perception of the trilogy as the complete manual that defines the righteous way of life meant that Muslims were reluctant to embrace new ideas. This meant that the religion of Islam was not easy to reform. Indeed, whenever external forces challenged Islamic nations, the cry for embracing "true" Islam as defined in the trilogy dominated. This situation continues today, with the likes of Bin Laden calling for the establishment of "true" Islam internally and invoking jihad to Islamize the world. This is unlike other major religions—Christianity, Buddhism or Hinduism, where external influences can be credited with creating reform.

In the next few pages the practice and evolution of Islam is analyzed to determine how we should deal with political Islam.

Disappearing Non-Muslims

If political Islamic ideology is cleverly designed for violent conquest, most material in Islamic trilogy should talk about jihad as war. Indeed, over 50 percent of the Medina Koran deals with hypocrites and jihad against unbelievers. Nearly 75 percent of Sira deals with jihad. About 97 percent of the Hadith recorded by Bukhari is about war.[5] The trilogy commends Islam as the perfect political system, destined to rule the world for all times. Starting with Medina, Islam has spread almost always by the sword in many continents. In the lands it has occupied, indigenous cultures, religions, and in many instances, languages, have disappeared.

William Warner notes:

> [Political] Islam has been waging civilizational war for centuries. Before Muslims arrived, Egypt and North Africa and the southern coast of the Mediterranean were Christian. There was a Buddhist monastery in Alexandria, Egypt. Turkey was Buddhist and Christian. Persia—now Iran— was Zoroastrian. The Hindu culture covered an area of the world twice as large as it is now. Languages disappeared to be replaced by Arabic. When Napoleon invaded Egypt, he had discovered that the Muslim population knew nothing about the pyramids or temples. The 5,000 old culture of the Pharaohs had been annihilated.[58]

Islam in Middle Age

A 14th century influential Islamic scholar, Ibn Taymiyya, had shaped the idea of what jihad meant and put it in the context of Islamic law. He belonged to the *Hanbali* school of thought, which is among the four orthodox Sunni schools of jurisprudence. He lived at a time when Shamanist Mongols had conquered the core of the Muslim world. Also, he elevated the importance of waging jihad, making it even more important than some of the customary five obligatory duties of Muslims. For him the purpose of jihad was to fight until all religion was for God alone. He also suggested fighting Muslims who tried to avoid participating in jihad. He declared that unbelievers had to be fought and killed.[59]

Even the Sufi movement, heralded for its tolerance and mysticism, is not immune to the call for jihad. This is even seen in the 12th-century writings of Al-Ghazali, who is considered the paragon of the Sufi movement.[57]

During the time the Ottoman Islamic empire was entering a period of military reverses, in the middle of 18th century, Abd al-Wahhab started articulating his vision of Islam. An adherent to the *Hanbali* school of thought, he was clearly influenced by Ibn Taymiyya. Like his predecessor Taymiyya, Wahhab too prescribed jihad against fellow Muslim heretics as the solution to their evil. He also suggested that only God is worthy of worship, and in his view any Muslim worshiping images, idols, tombs, or shrines should be treated as unbelievers and should be fought and killed.[60] The Wahhabi Islam is still in practice and is identified as the predominant Islam of present day Saudi Arabia.

In India, toward the twilight of Mughal rule in the 16th century, scholar Shah Wali Allah called for forcing Islam on Hindus for their own well-being.[61] In Africa, political Islamists, Muhammed al-Jaylani, Usman dan Fodio and Shehu Ahmadu took to jihad aimed at restoring "true" Islam.[61]

Islam in Modern Age

Toward the end of 19th century, the Muslim elite felt weak in front of European powers. They were determined to extricate themselves from European domination and to return to their former military "glory". At first, in the beginning of the twentieth century, nationalist, socialist, and liberal Muslims helped form modern Muslim nations. But, overcome by centuries of underdevelopment, the progress was slow in achieving parity with Christian-majority West. This frustrated the Muslim public. Extremist Muslim scholars stepped in to fill the vacuum by asserting that a deeper embrace of the way of life defined in the trilogy would help Muslims to regain Muslim glory (it is not often pointed out what this glory is; it usually means conquest of unbelievers and their land). These scholars were: Muhammad Rashid Rida, Hassan al-Bana, Sayyid Abdul A'la Mawdudi, and Sayyid Qutb. Muhammad Rida is one generation ahead of the other three. In Mary Habeck's opinion:

> During the mid-twentieth century three ideologues (Al-Banna, Mawdudi and Qutb) would take the ideas of Ibn Taymiyya, Wahhab and Rida and transform them into a coherent set of beliefs about Islam, politics and warfare. Their thought is by far the most significant source of jihadi ideology as well as far other, less radical, expressions of Islamism.[62]

There are reasons for the near-absence of reform or moderation in Islam. Throughout history, even during modern times, those who articulated views the moderate side of Islam faced violence from entrenched extremist schools of Islamic thought. As discussed before, many Islamic scholars, including Ibn Taymiyya and Abd al-Wahhab, proposed waging war on fellow Muslim "heretics". Minority sects, such as

Ahamadiya Muslims, have faced persecution or even death at the hands of majority Sunni sects of Islam.

The emphasis on jihad in the trilogy meant that internal wealth creation is not among the priorities. Hence, conquest or jihad-building is an important means of generating new wealth and status within the community. But the modern age is characterized by materialism, which requires wealth creation. In essence, this defines the fundamental incompatibility of Islamic states in the global order.

In ancient times, campaigns in the name of religions were common. This is true of Christianity, the world's largest religion and the archrival of Islam. But the Christianity of today is not a religion of conquest through violence. Most Western nations have a Christian majority and yet practice secularism. In nations where followers of other major faiths (such as Buddhism or Hinduism) live, the societies are by and large secular. However, in many nations where Muslims are a majority, political Islam is the dominating power and exerts strong influence over governance.

In most Islamic nations, non-Muslims are treated as second-class citizens or residents (examples would be Saudi Arabia, Pakistan, and Iran). The origin of this outlook is traced to the core of Islam—the trilogy.[5] Notably, many Islamic nations have disappearing minorities.

As is discussed in next chapter, South Asia is a region of particular focus in political Islam's conquest through jihad. In every area of South Asia, once Muslims obtained power through majority status, be it in Pakistan, Bangladesh, or the Kashmir valley, massive ethnic cleansing and marginalizing of non-Muslims has been observed. In fact, most of Pakistan has been cleansed off non-Muslims, and the same has happened in the Kashmir valley. Bangladesh is well on its way (Chapter Three). One objective and important conclusion can be made on the basis of this data: political Islam as practiced in South Asia doesn't believe in coexistence of differing religions even in modern times. This data, unique in exposing the outlook of political Islam when Muslims become majority, indicates a bleak future for non-Muslims, as Muslim populations rise faster than the non-Muslim populations in non-Muslim majority nations.

In Malaysia, a barely Muslim majority nation at the time of independence has since systematically worked to marginalize its non-Muslim citizens. When they can, ethnic Chinese and Indians have been steadily filing out of the country. In Egypt, Coptic Christians, who have been resident natives for a thousand years and are often targeted by the Muslim Brotherhood, are moving out.

When Muslims are a minority in non-Muslim nations, conquest through warfare or constitution-based discrimination by the majority is unlikely due to Muslim minority status. Hence, from a conquest point of view, the percentage of Muslims in the population must be raised. This is happening in many nations—France, Britain, India, Russia, and even Israel. But Muslim clerics have cooperated with the regimes in power in Muslim majority states to help convince their followers to have smaller families.[63] This has not been done in nations such as India, for obvious reasons.

Here is the most important question of all: what will happen to non-Muslim majority nations once their resident Muslims achieve majority? The answer to this question, this book contends, should determine the policy approach to the war on terror.

Science to the Rescue

As condemned unbelievers in the view of adherents of political Islam, we have every reason to scientifically investigate the origin and the contents of the Islamic trilogy.[64]

- o The Koran was the first book of the trilogy to be put together, and that was done several decades after the death of Mohammed.[8] In a Hadith it is said that Koranic verses were collected from bits of bone, stone, parchment, date palm leaves, and also from the memories of those who had memorized it.[65]

This is evidence that it is very likely that the Koran was not accurately put together, nor it is complete.

- o It is mentioned by Said in his Hadith that at least one verse was missed. It was found in Khuzaima's possession.[65]

One wonders how many more Koranic verses went missing. This is proof that the Koran is not complete. If it is not complete, how valid is the interpretation that the Koran is the word of God?

- o Mohammed himself was prone to forgetfulness. B6,61,562: Mohammed listened to a man reciting the Koran, and he says: "May Allah bless that man. He has reminded me of verses and chapters I had forgotten".[66]

This brings up the legitimate argument that Mohammed could have forgotten the original "God's revelations" as well.

- o When Mohammed conquered Mecca while riding with an army from Medina, he gave a specific order to kill a man. He was a former secretary. He had earlier accused Mohammed of letting him enter a better speech when he was recording Mohammed's Koranic revelations.[67]

This apparently caused the secretary to lose faith in Mohammed and move away. This narrative in the Hadith gives the impression of portions of the Koran being doctored even during the time of Mohammed.

- o In many situations when Mohammed made "revelations", as described in the Koran, Hadith or Sira, careful note-takers do not appear to be present.

This means the revelations were written down later. This raises concern about the verses' authenticity.

Mistreatment by God, the Merciful

- o On the treatment of Muslim women: 34th verse of the fourth chapter of the Koran, *An-Nisa*, or Women: "[A]nd (as to) those on whose part you fear desertion, admonish them and leave them alone in the sleeping-places and beat them,".[68]
- o Koranic verses such as *At-Tauba* ("The Repentance") 9:5, state that Muslims should "slay the pagans wherever ye find them".[68]
- o On how Muslims should treat Christians and Jews: *Al-Mâ'idah* ("The Table Spread with Food") 5:51 states: "Take not the Jews and Christians as friends".[68]

All of the above reveal the conquest-based and political emphasis of the ideology: death for non-Muslims such as Buddhists or Hindus, dislike of Christians and Jews, and double standards for fellow Muslims—the mothers and daughters of today's and tomorrow's Muslims.

Make no mistake. These are not just ancient writings; they are a way of everyday life that is practiced by communities and nations. The Taliban-ruled Afghanistan was one such nation.

Even if "God's revelations" had been made to Mohammed, based on the information presented in the trilogy there is an open question as to how accurately these revelations were taken down, preserved and converted in the form of books or any other form of information storage. We know from archeological studies that as recently as a thousand years ago humans lacked credible technology for processing and storing information. Clearly, leaves, stones, bits of bone, and people's memory are not reliable forms of note-taking or information storage when Mohamed delivered his "revelations". This is common sense!

This angle raises serious doubts about the credibility of *sharia*, which is considered Muslim personal law and derived from the Koran.

Mohammed may have delivered a revelation from his deathbed calling for reconciliation, along the lines described in the Meccan Koran, in order to make permanent peace with unbelievers. However, his immediate followers may have concealed it to keep the power base. The point is, where does one draw the line regarding the accuracy or completeness of the Koran, and on what grounds? For something as profound as God's "revelations," there shouldn't be an iota of doubt about its authenticity. This is clearly not the case here.

Another relevant issue is whether the Arab tribes Mohammed belonged to had the ability to identify phony messengers of God. After all, many in ancient history claimed to possess God's revelations. But most were laughed off. "Messengers" of God distinguished themselves by their claim of supernatural abilities, such as receiving God's revelations or possessing supernatural powers.

Modern science provides an understanding of nature and explanations for natural phenomena that were considered supernatural or "Godly" just centuries ago. This implies that as a society increases its scientific awareness, it can more easily distinguish phony messengers of God.

How good was the scientific understanding of the tribes Mohammed belonged to?

To build an extensive understanding of nature or science requires sophisticated experimental verification. This is common sense—a scientific explanation must be verified in real life. An understanding of our solar system may require a powerful telescope, but it requires industrial know-how to build one. The more we want to understand the science of the solar system, the more sophisticated are the necessary instruments—radio telescopes, rockets, satellites etc. All of this requires considerable infrastructure. The conclusion is that to conduct a thorough verification, a society requires increasingly complex infrastructure.

But we know from archeological studies that the Saudi tribes Mohammed was part of didn't have sophisticated infrastructure, which meant that their understanding of nature or science was limited. The conclusion that follows from this? Arab tribes at the time of Mohammed were not well-placed to identify phony messengers of God or falsehood.

Inability to Coexist

William Warner defines the Golden Rule of unitary ethics, and outlines why violations of this ethic have made it becomes impossible to coexist with political Islam:

> On the basis of the Golden Rule—the equality of human beings—we have created democracy, ended slavery and treat women and men as political equals. So the Golden Rule is a unitary ethic. All people are to be treated the same. All religions have some version of the Golden Rule except Islam...The term "human being" has no meaning inside of Islam. There is no such thing as humanity, only the duality of the believer and unbeliever. Look at the ethical statements found in the Hadith. A Muslim should not lie, cheat, kill or steal from other Muslims. But a Muslim may lie, deceive or kill an unbeliever if it advances Islam.
>
> There is no such thing as a universal statement of ethics in Islam. Muslims are to be treated one way and unbelievers another way. The closest Islam comes to a universal statement of ethics is that the entire world must submit to Islam... By the way, this dualistic ethic is the basis for jihad. The ethical system sets up the unbeliever as less than human and therefore, it is easy to kill, harm or deceive the unbeliever.

The dualism of Islam is more deceitful and offers two choices on how to treat the unbeliever. The unbeliever can be treated nicely, in the same way a farmer treats his cattle well. So Islam can be "nice", but in no case is the unbeliever a "brother" or a friend. In fact, there are some 14 verses of the Koran that are emphatic—a Muslim is never a friend to the unbeliever. A Muslim may be "friendly," but he is never an actual friend. And the degree to which a Muslim is actually a true friend is the degree to which he is not a Muslim, but (considered) a hypocrite.[5]

The inability of political Islam to coexist with other religions or their followers is traced to the Islamic trilogy, which is probably designed to ensure conquest. Still, the proof is in the pudding.

How do most Muslim societies who have embraced the trilogy deal with unbelievers? Through jihad. The next chapter sheds light on jihad waged on unbelievers.

Chapter Three

Many a Face of Jihad

In Muslim nations under a strong political Islamic influence, the citizens' aspiration is one of conquest for Islam. The primary national agenda is waging jihad on non-Muslim nations by indoctrinating their resident Muslims and sending home-grown jihadis to fight these nations. Indeed, across the globe, many nations with sizable minority Muslim populations have been victimized by jihad. In this chapter, three select nations or regions—Israel, Europe and India—where Muslims are a minority are studied in order to understand how various forms of jihad are executed.

Gangster Al Capone was found guilty on a relatively minor tax evasion charge, not on many heinous crimes he had allegedly committed. The gangster nations of the world—the axis of jihad nations—may have been more circumspect in the acts of terror they have directed at powerful nations of the world, but with soft or weak states such as India, they didn't have to. In fact, India has been a perennial victim of political Islam. These soft-victim nations of jihad may possess some of the most incisive data implicating the gangster nations. Due to this incentive, this book takes a critical look at India in order to provide wealth of jihad-related data and analysis that is not yet widely known or realized.

Assault on Israel

Among the nations bordering Islamic states, Israel, along with India, is the nation most targeted by political Islam. As it is a developed nation and a close ally of America, Israel has been able to ward off military attacks from neighboring Islamic states and their proxies effectively thus far. But the emergence of Nasrallah's Hizbollah and Iran's effort to acquiring nuclear weapons has likely made Israel more vulnerable than it has been since its birth.

There are compelling reasons to view the warfare imposed by Israel's Arab neighbors as an extension of the war started by Islam's founder, Mohammed, about 1400 years ago. The trilogy talks about Jewish settlements in the heart of Saudi Arabia and in nearby lands, and Mohammed's verbal and armed conflicts with them.[69,70] In fact, for quite some time, Saudi Arabia has had virtually no Jewish population. It can be argued, based upon the trilogy, that political Islam didn't have any particular liking for Jews. Clearly, the Jewish community has suffered grievously in Saudi Arabia. In addition to a substantial presence in Palestine, Jews had lived in many Middle Eastern nations for centuries. This, along with various historical documents and archeological studies, point to the reality: Jews belong in the Middle East. In the aftermath of the Nazi holocaust, it is only natural that Jews would want a land and nation in the Middle East to call their own.

The establishment of a modern Jewish state in the 1940s led to the displacement of a large number of Palestinians. There was also another side of the story not widely noted—the ensuing Israel-Arab conflict led to a large number of Jews leaving Arab countries for Israel.[71]

Very few Arab Muslim states have recognized Israel's right to exist thus far. Even Egypt's recognition, in light of its otherwise unfriendly outlook, can only be seen as an act of convenience, designed to get large handouts from America, than one of conviction. Muslim nations' denial of Israel's right to exist, the continued one-sided harping of displaced Palestinians while ignoring the displacement of Jews from Arab lands, and the funding of a slew of suicide bombers who have wrecked thousands of Jewish families, give the impression of systematic war crimes committed on a large scale. Going by the nature of these crimes and their massive scale, these appear to be crimes against humanity whose intention is to drive Jews out from the land of Israel and to expand or recapture the land for political Islam, as is described in the trilogy.

Political Islam's grip on Palestinians is evident by the power and influence of hateful and retrogressive Muslim clergies. The clerical preaching does not appear to emphasize the need for Palestinians to focus on modern education or on learning to work with Israelis. Instead, the emphasis has been on building feelings of grievance in impressionable minds. This means nation-building is on the backburner, while jihad-building is emphasized. These are among the primary reasons that the enormous aid that has been given to the Palestinians by the Europeans, Americans, and even Arabs has not been used constructively. The extent of political Islam's influence can be ascertained by the 2006 election results, in which Hamas, an offshoot of the Muslim Brotherhood, was voted to power in the West Bank and Gaza. Hamas' manifesto is extremist and is dedicated to the destruction of Israel.[72]

Unless Palestinians are liberated from political Islam, there is little possibility of peace. The bulging population, which is due to a high Palestinian growth rate, creates a steady stream of jihadis to sustain the conflict with Israel.

The European Survival Threat

Wealthy European nations, which are among the most advanced in the world, still found themselves too slow to react to the emerging threat from political Islam. Not only do Muslims in Europe have much higher reproduction rate compared to the natives, but they appear to be firmly in thrall to political Islam. Among the most vulnerable nations are France and the Netherlands, with Britain, Belgium, and Germany following closely. Muslims in France constitute about 12 percent of the total population. However, in terms of newborns, Muslim percentage rate is probably close to a whopping 30 percent, aided by low birth rate of the white natives. In the nearby Netherlands, the Muslim population is at 6 percent, and probably has a much higher growth rate compared to the native whites.[73,74] Overall, among newborns, the Muslim percentage in Europe is estimated to be anywhere between 15 to 20 percent.[73]

Colonial connections and the need for cheap manpower led to the initial wave of immigration from Muslim nations to Europe. Later on, Muslims' close family relatives, including relatives by marriage, were allowed to settle in Europe. The Middle Eastern funding for Wahhabi preaching in European mosques aggravated assimilation problems for the Muslim immigrants and even their European-born children. Clerics who knew little English were allowed to be imported from Islamic nations with strong political Islamic bases and influence. Clearly, these clerics must have had little or no idea of community-building in western nations, but as torch-bearers of political Islam they sure know one thing: jihad-building.

In the Netherlands, Theo van Gogh's gruesome murder by an Islamist underlined the gravity of the situation. Van Gogh's murder was the final straw for many Dutch white families who were concerned about growing Islamic extremism. Many of them have left for Canada, Australia, and New Zealand. Survey results in April 2005 showed that every third Dutchman wanted to leave the country.[75] A July 2005 poll found 22 percent of British Muslims saying past summer's rush-hour bombings of London's metro system, which killed 52 people, were justified because of Britain's support for the war on terror. This included 31 percent of young British Muslims.[76] In France, the Interior Ministry accused Muslims of waging an undeclared "intifada" against police, with attacks injuring an average of 14 officers a day.[77] The large-scale riots by French Muslims pointed out not just their assimilation inadequacies, but also the jihadist outlook and intentions of large sections of French Muslim population.[78]

A study conducted by the right-wing think tank 'Policy Exchange' has found that 40 percent of Muslims between the ages of 16 and 24 said they would prefer to live under *sharia* law in Britain, a legal system based on the teachings of the Koran. The figure among the over-55 age group, in contrast, was only 17 percent. Munira Mirza, the broadcaster and one of the authors of the report, was quoted as saying that multicultural policies pursued by the Government had succeeded in making things worse rather than better. "The emergence of a strong Muslim identity in Britain is, in part, a result of multi-cultural policies implemented since the 1980s which have emphasized difference at the expense of shared national identity and divided people along ethnic, religious and cultural lines."[79]

Before blaming the locals for not helping Muslims to assimilate, one should study other transplanted communities. This apparent "negative influence" of multi-culturalism has not occurred in Hindu or Sikh communities, whose members started arriving from India in 1950s as blue-collar workers to work in British textile mills. These émigrés shared language, food habits, history and some culture with Muslims from Pakistan who too arrived at about the same time to share work. Yet almost 30-40 years later, Hindus and Sikhs have income levels either comparable to or surpassing those of native whites; their children have excelled in education, at times even surpassing the majority.[80] Muslims of Pakistani origin have exactly the opposite record; they tend to be poorer, less educated, and to have high crime rates.[79] Three of the four bombers associated with the 7/7 London bombings were from ethnic Pakistani Muslim communities.[81] The reason has now become transparent: political Islam rules these Muslims, just as it does in Pakistan.

Living the "European dream"—a comfortable, gadget-oriented life that requires wealth and that prepares children to succeed through good education—meant that for a resident, children have become expensive responsibility both in terms of time and resources. Understandably, the European socialist system gave generous subsidies to the poor and especially to those who have many children. This policy was a godsend for political Islam. Not material-minded but conquest-minded, clerics encouraged Muslims to have more children and to receive government subsidies. In Denmark, 5 percent of the Muslim population receives 40 percent of welfare outlays.[82]

European Muslim families are told by the clerics to reject the European dream and instead embrace a tribal Arabic way of life. This has led to high Muslim growth rates, and a parenthood that disowned certain responsibility towards its children and instead transferred it to imported radical Muslim clerics. This has resulted in a new generation of home-grown European jihadis under clerical control.

Why did European societies, especially the ruling class, fail to wake up to this growing genocidal threat decades ago? As former rulers of the Islamic nations from which most of the Muslims emigrated, the European ruling class never saw them as challenging at any point. Bruce Bawer explains how the emerging Islamist threat went unnoticed for decades: in the Western Europe those who reach high office have been active in party politics since they were very young. "You learn to fit in. You learn not to rock the boat... Those who are most lavishly rewarded tend to be those who play the strongest loyalty to the party and its platforms. Original thinkers are not welcome. People who might shake things up are closed out."[83] Normally the liberal press gave a sympathetic ear to Muslim leaders who made claims of harassment and of being disadvantaged—a classic tactic of political Islam, calling itself a victim even as it victimizes unbelievers.

Not many had understood that political Islam was experiencing a resurgence due to the free wealth in the form of oil; nor was it understood that it is conquest-oriented. Some clear-headed politicians—Pim Fortuyn of the Netherlands, for instance—who boldly pointed out the "Muslim problem" found themselves in an unenviable position—in fear of being unfairly crucified by the media with descriptions such as "racist," "bigot," etc.

In an operation that is typical of the way political Islam is making inroads into Europe, Paul Belien analyzes how extremists are taking control of Muslim population in Belgium:

About three years ago, young men dressed in black moved into the neighborhoods. They had been trained in Saudi Arabia and Jordan and adhere to Salafism, a radical version of Islam. They set up youth organizations, which gradually took over the local mosques. "The Salafists know how to debate and they know the Qur'an by heart, while the elderly running the mosques do not," she said They also have money. "One of them told me that he gets Saudi funds." Because they are eloquent, the radicals soon became the official spokesmen of the Muslim community, also in dealing with the city authorities... the reason why the Socialists, who run the city, allow the Islamists to do as they please is because they want to get the Muslim vote, which is controlled increasingly by the Salafists who are in the process of taking over the mosques.[84]

Many European nations, including France and the Netherlands, are struggling to come up with an effective policy framework to deal with political Islamic threat. Given the circumstances, the European Union's unease regarding Turkey's inclusion is entirely understandable. Allowing Turkey to become part of Europe could be one of the fastest ways to empower and even ensure political Islam's dominance of Europe. Turkey is an overwhelmingly Muslim-majority nation, with a large and growing population. The letter by the author that was published in the *Washington Times* gives the EU's perspective:

Why the EU does not want Turkey

In their column "Road map to a Western Turkey" (Commentary, yesterday), John C. Hulsman and Brett D. Schaefer have glossed over an important concern many Europeans have about Turkey's inclusion in the European Union: namely, giving Turkey's Muslim population easier access to settling in Europe.

European Muslims, including second-generation ones, have difficulty assimilating and are among the largest recipients of welfare. They also have high crime rates and poor education levels. While the native white population in the European Union is barely reproducing itself, European Muslims have among the highest birth rates.

If Turkey were admitted to the union, Europe's Muslims could jump from about 4 percent to 20 percent of the population. Furthermore, there is the obvious issue of pan-Islamic extremism sweeping the world, including Europe, with the burgeoning of the immigrant Muslim population. It also must be acknowledged that, given its deep Islamic roots, Turkey is at best an experiment in democracy and modern development. Its admission into the European Union could portend the devastation of Western Europe through a massive influx of Muslims who have little in common with Europeans.[85]

As the resident Muslim population under the control of political Islam rapidly increases vis-à-vis the native population in Western Europe, the democracies of these countries are coming under an increasing Islamic siege, making it difficult for them to fight back.[86] The situation in India, discussed in the following section, gives a grim picture how such a siege will evolve and what it means for Europe.

Siege of India

It is no exaggeration to note that India stands today as an advanced laboratory for Project Jihad. Supported by Saudi Arabia, Pakistan has made deep inroads into the fabric of Indian society. This section offers insights into how a political Islamic siege of a non-Muslim developing nation is carried out. Incisive data on the impact of jihad is presented here. This description of what is happening to India in the hands of political Islam and of the fate of non-Muslims in India's neighbors should be eye-opening.

All available evidence suggests that India is engulfed by a multi-front jihad. To understand this assault on India, one has to look at the larger picture associated with Islamic conquest in South Asia itself. South Asia is the region where political Islam's border ends and pluralism, as represented by secular Indian democracy, begins.

The Islamic thrust into ancient India started within a few hundred years after the death of Mohammed. Muslim victories led to the establishment of kingdoms in vast portions of ancient Hindu-majority India; this continued until the advent of the British. Despite ruling most of India for several hundred years, Muslim conquerors from Middle East or their descendents could manage to convert only a small fraction of native Hindus to Islam. This is due to the fact that Hinduism is divided into disparate groups, each with their own ideologies, and to the small number of the Muslim ruling elite as compared to the vast Hindu population in extended areas. It also made little economic sense to exterminate Hindus, when as slaves they could well serve the Muslim ruling class.

Still, history records millions of Hindus and Sikhs killed by Muslim invaders and kings in India; their temples deliberately and systematically destroyed.[87,88]

When British East India Company entered India several hundred years ago, the long Muslim rule was in its twilight. Hindu and Sikh kings were in the process of successfully transplanting Muslim kings. After a series of decisive battles, the powerful British established supremacy. Still, even during British rule, the Muslim elite saw themselves as rulers of Hindus. However, Indian Muslims were falling behind, due to their reluctance to embrace modern education. Apart from their comprising over 25 percent of manpower in the Indian military under the British, Muslims had dismal representation in most government sectors.[89]

When the ruling British colonizers decided to leave India, not wanting to be dominated by Hindu majority, some Muslims demanded a land where Muslims were the majority. In an election conducted before the independence in 1947, Indian Muslims overwhelmingly voted for a separate nation.[90] British India was partitioned in the year 1947 into Hindu-majority India and Muslim-majority Pakistan. The 25-30 percent Muslim population in British India got 25 percent of the land, in the form of East and West Pakistans.[91] Minorities were expected to stay in their respective lands even after the partition. It is illustrative to note what Mohammed Ali Jinnah, the founder of Pakistan, said before Pakistan was formed:

I shall not depart from what I have said repeatedly with regard to minorities. The minorities, to whichever community they may belong, will be safe-guarded. Their religion or their faith or belief will be protected in every way possible. Their life and property will be secure. There will be no interference of any kind with the freedom of worship. They will have their property and culture. They will be in all respects treated as citizens of Pakistan without any distinction of caste, religion or creed.[92]

However, within the next four years, spearheaded by mosques, most non-Muslims—primarily Hindus and Sikhs who constituted at least 20 percent of the population—were driven out of West Pakistan, and hundreds of thousands were possibly killed (it is now called Pakistan).[93] Now the non-Muslim population there stands at less than 2 percent.[94] This was achieved once the Muslim majority in Pakistan achieved political power by obtaining independence from the British. Also, some non-Muslim Pakistanis converted to Islam in order to keep their property and not live as hounded "infidels" in this new Islamic nation.

Indian Punjab, which shares a border with Pakistani Punjab, retaliated by driving out Muslims from its region. However, in the rest of India, most Muslims were allowed to stay. According to Indian census report of 1951, 10 percent of the Indian population consisted of Muslims.[95]

At that time Saudi Arabia was a poor nation and was in no position to influence these events. Here is evidence indicating that even without the help of oil-based resources or the support of a wealthy and influential Saudi Arabia, political Islam in the modern age can be genocidal.

Prior to 1947, East Pakistan—now called Bangladesh—had at least 29 percent Hindu and Buddhist population. This has now been reduced to less than 10 percent.[93] These minorities, in the aftermath of the partition, while certainly not violently kicked out as in West Pakistan, were finding conditions slowly deteriorating for them in the Muslim majority nation. There has been a steady outflow of non-Muslims from East Pakistan into India.

The government of both West and East Pakistans was located in West Pakistan. Urdu, a language spoken mostly in the West and based upon Arabic script, was the official language, although East Pakistanis were more numerical and spoke Bengali, which is a language based on Sanskrit and is considered a Hindu or an "infidel" language. The West Pakistanis dominated the military and the government bureaucracy. The cultural and power-sharing disagreements between the two Pakistans resulted in West Pakistan sending its troops to crush the East Pakistani rebellion and, importantly, to eradicate what it saw as a "infidel" Hindu influence on East Pakistan. The West Pakistani troops selectively chose Hindus to rape and murder, and drove out millions of Hindus and Bengali Muslims into India (Chapter One, Section: *Axis of Jihad*). This led to the Indo-Pak war of 1971; as a result of this, East Pakistan gained the independence to eventually become Islamic Bangladesh.

In recent years, more Hindus and Buddhists have left Bangladesh for India. Their community leaders have consistently complained of violence directed at them by Islamic parties and groups, especially by *Jamat-e-Islami*, which was originally established by none other than the well-known jihadist scholar of South Asia, Abdul A'la Mawdudi. At a 2006 terrorism conference in Bombay, a minority leader from Bangladesh implicated both Pakistan and Saudi Arabia in funding extremist organizations.[35] Many powerful people in these nations have been eyeing India's North-Eastern region for an Islamic conquest. To achieve this vision, they have been sending Muslim Bangladeshis through the porous Indian borders for some time. By some estimates there are at least some 10 million illegal Bangladeshi Muslims in India.[96]

What about Muslim growth within India? The Indian Muslim population has increased from 10 percent in 1951 to 13.5 percent in 2001.[95] The Kashmir valley, a Muslim-majority region within a non-Muslim-majority India, has seen massive non-Muslim ethnic cleansing. In 1989, over 300,000 Hindus were driven out to the rest of India.[93] Even towns that have a Muslim majority but that lie within regions having over 90 percent non-Muslim populations in India are not immune from the desire for jihad. The Thondi and Rasathipuram Municipalities of Ramanathapuram and Vellore districts in the southern state of Tamilnadu are in non-Muslim majority areas. These Muslim-ruled municipalities denied the minority Hindu areas civic amenities, funding for schools, garbage clearing, etc., and sent notices in Urdu bluntly telling them to convert to Islam if they wanted civic facilities. Non-Muslims have found themselves driven out of the Muslim majority cities of Meerut and Mau in northern India.[97]

These statistics, which are hardly known, shows political Islam's crimes directed at humanity, especially in modern times. This brutal treatment of fellow humans for the purposes of conquest and Islamization of the lands can be traced to the trilogy (Chapter Two). What is striking is the deadly influence of a political ideology masquerading as a religion. Indeed, about 25 percent of what was known as the British India has now become almost exclusively Muslim, or are on their way to becoming so. Non-Muslims are now squeezed into present-day India. As a result of this non-Muslim ethnic cleansing in all Muslim-majority areas of South Asia, India had to accommodate about 85 percent of the pre-1947 population in about 75 percent of the land.

These statistics show that even during modern times in South Asia, it is not possible to coexist with political Islam. Political Islam grows in power along with Muslim population, and it can achieve absolute power when Muslims are in majority. These are exactly the kinds of power statistics needed to undertake decisive and long-term policy measures and to help mobilize non-Muslims.

The proliferation of *madarasas* in Pakistan is well-known. It started occurring only in the late 1970s, when Middle Eastern petrodollars started flowing into Pakistan. Nevertheless, Pakistan's preference for Islamism goes all the way back to its inception. Since 1947, Punjab University, based in Lahore, has granted over 60 percent of its doctoral degrees in subjects related to Islam; in contrast, only a few percent of its doctoral degrees have been given in engineering.[98] It was only in March 2006 that Pakistan decided to establish premier engineering institutions.[99] In contrast, India went on to form several Indian institutes of technology and regional engineering colleges in 1950s and 1960s. Undoubtedly, this education initiative has played a crucial role in India's economic resurgence and wealth creation, and is particularly related to India's software successes.[100]

With this emphasis on Islamism and Islamic history and its focus on Islamic conquest, it is not hard to see why Pakistan's primary goal is expanding political Islam's boundaries, rather than nation-building.

Having managed to get rid of most of its unbeliever population quickly by 1950, Pakistan had carried out the first stage of Islamic conquest. The Islam-oriented constitution undermined and marginalized the leftover non-Muslims in Pakistan and laws were enacted discriminating against non-Muslims in the hope that non-Muslims would either convert to Islam or leave its land. With the Muslims of old India holding power in Pakistan, it is also a natural base for regaining the past glory of Muslim "conquest" of a "Hindu" India. Outmatched by India economically and militarily, Islamic Pakistan has turned to a multi-faceted jihad to weaken India, using Indian Muslims as foot-soldiers and sending into India its home-grown jihadis nurtured through a farm system of *madarasas*.[34] It has bankrolled several Middle Eastern nations, Saudi Arabia in particular, to indoctrinate Indian Muslims with extreme versions of political Islamic ideology.

With Middle Eastern aid and Pakistan's logistics, Muslim populations in neighboring Nepal, Bangladesh and even Srilanka have also been fed extremist versions of political Islamic ideology or theology through newly established mosques and *madarasas*.[101] This has made Muslim majority Bangladesh increasingly accepting of extending political Islam's frontiers. Faced with less penetrable borders with India, according to Indian reports, Pakistan has used Islamic Bangladesh's porous borders to infiltrate terrorists into India.

Pakistan's crowning strategic and jihad success lies in establishing a terror base within India through the Muslim Kashmir insurgency. What is notable is Pakistan's support for "self-determination" of Muslims in Indian Kashmir, even as the Pakistani part of Kashmir is almost completely cleansed off non-Muslims—with most driven away to India. This approach is consistent with trying to expand political Islam's frontiers, at the expense of non-Muslims.

Under Musharraf, Pakistan-influenced terrorists have killed scores of Hindu families, and have successfully created a Hindu exodus out of certain parts of Kashmir.[102] To put more pressure on India to give up Kashmir to Pakistan, under Musharraf, Pakistan-sponsored terrorists are suspected to have escalated acts of terror in the rest of India. These escalating terror attacks have imposed a huge economic cost on an impoverished nation, and have indirectly undermined humanity in India. These attacks have escalated, despite the promise given by Musharraf in the following joint statement released on January 6, 2004 in India: "[H]e [Musharraf] will not permit any territory under Pakistan's control to be used to support terrorism in any manner."[103]

Seen in the above context, Musharraf's consistent declaration that "it [Pakistan] has a political and moral right to support what it calls a struggle for self-determination in Indian-controlled Kashmir" has become an immoral and genocidal framework for extending Islam's frontiers.[104] This is through a combination of non-Muslim ethnic cleansing—a form of genocide—and support for self-determination of Muslims, which in reality has turned out to be terror sponsorship. Having already worked to indoctrinate Kashmiri Muslims a hatred of Hindu-majority India, Pakistan hopes that, given the right to self-determination, Muslim-majority Indian Kashmir will vote to join Pakistan, along with the land.

There is more to the Kashmir Muslim insurgency than a violent confrontation between political Islamists and the Indian state. This insurgency appears to be part of a much larger operation to indoctrinate the local Muslim population in order to extend political Islam's boundaries. *Jamait-e-Islami* operates several hundred *madarasas* in Indian Kashmir, with funds coming from Saudi Arabia and other Muslim nations. The Kashmiri *Jamait* is an extension of the outfit operating out of Pakistan. *Jamait* managed to instill virulent hatred of "infidel" India in the minds of young children, in order to initiate indoctrination at a young age. Below is a portion of a school poem prescribed for Class III:

Little children, be very calm
I will tell you what is Islam
You may be a few and without army,
But you must fight for Islam.[105]

Kashmir has become a terror base for political Islam within India. Its Muslim population has been strategically indoctrinated to become sympathetic to political Islamic cause in order to sponsor terrorists infiltrating from Pakistan. Understanding jihad in Kashmir is important, as jihad in the rest of India is developing along in similar lines.

Geographically and demographically, Kashmir is divided into three regions within India. The fertile Kashmir valley consists mostly of Sunni Muslims, who make up roughly 50 percent of the total Kashmir population. Jammu is mostly Hindu, and Ladakh has a ratio of about 55 percent Buddhist to 45 percent Muslim residents.[106] As it is India's only Muslim majority state, the Muslim Kashmir ruling elite extracted a special status for Kashmir through Article 370 of Indian Constitution. Under this deal, the Indian constitution and laws are not applicable in Kashmir. As well, people from the rest of India could not buy property in Kashmir, but Kashmiris could do so in the rest of India.[107] Although Article 370 was meant to be a temporary provision, it is still applicable.

New Delhi's undemocratic means of excluding radical or secessionist leaders from power contributed to Muslim Kashmiri grievance. However, the religion-based grievances nurtured by the Kashmir Muslim leadership for several decades comprised the primary ingredient needed for Pakistan to implement the Afghan model of jihad in Kashmir. Starting in the 1980s, this involved setting up *madarasas* or mosques inside Kashmir to instill elements of Wahhabism or Deobandism (an early Indian version of Wahhabism) and a hatred of "infidel" India in minds of the local Muslim population. This could be accomplished because Kashmir had its own laws and its administration was in the hands of Kashmir valley Muslims, who are known for their sympathy to the cause of political Islam. Just as in Afghan jihad, many Middle Eastern nations were involved in funding this endeavor. Apparently, the goals of the Kashmir jihad are threefold: to cleanse the region of non-Muslims, to use Kashmir as a staging post to destabilize the rest of India, and to merge Kashmir with the greater Islamic world by attaching it to Pakistan.

As a natural first step toward Islamizing Kashmir, the conditions were being created to cleanse the Kashmir valley of its entire Hindu population. Newspapers and mosques in Kashmir valley openly exhorted Hindu "infidels" to leave Kashmir. Many mainstream mosques in Kashmir posted a list of local "infidel" Hindus to be killed or driven away. Sure enough, with killings of Hindus increasing and their businesses destroyed, over 300,000 Hindu minorities were forced to leave the Kashmir valley in 1989.[93] Many of their left over property have now been illegally grabbed.

Slow to react to the jihad buildup in Kashmir, New Delhi finally struck back forcefully after most Hindus were driven out of Kashmir valley. This conflict almost escalated into an Indo-Pak war in 1989. Since then Muslim insurgency has spread to other parts of Kashmir. Predictably, indiscriminate killings of Hindu civilians are now underway in the Doda region of Kashmir—35 Hindu children, women and men were massacred by suspected *LeT* terrorists on May 1, 2006—to create Hindu exodus from this part of Kashmir.[102]

Kashmir is now held together by the Indian army, with the help of several hundred thousand soldiers—a huge drain on India's limited resources. India does not appear to have a long-term plan to deal with political Islam's successful efforts to cleanse the region of non-Muslims.

While the ruling Kashmir valley Muslims claim grievances at the hands of India, it is pertinent to discuss how they treat non-Muslim areas within Kashmir. There is also the issue of the extent of grants extracted by them from the central government in New Delhi. If a seasoned reader thought that Kashmiri Muslims would use the bogey of "discrimination" to marginalize non-Muslim Kashmiri residents and expect India to subsidize their life style, he/she would be right on the mark. This is a classic behavior of a Muslim population under the grip of political Islam.

Indian journalist Arvind Lavakare, a columnist for *Rediff.com*, has pointed out in a detailed analysis that until 2005, for almost sixty years, the Chief Minister of Kashmir came only from Muslim-majority Kashmir valley. Through a pseudo-reservation system, Kashmir valley Muslims, who constitute 50 percent of the population, have grabbed about 75 percent of the positions in government, semi-government organizations, and in educational institutions all throughout the state of Kashmir. In Muslim-controlled Kashmir, admissions to educational institutions are not merit-based but are decided along religious lines. While Jammu and Ladakh contribute over 90 percent to the state's finances, only a small portion of these revenues are spent on the underdeveloped Jammu and Ladakh regions. This out-of-proportion pseudo-reservation for Kashmir valley Muslims, as well as the almost one-way collection of tax revenues, come at enormous expense to Hindu-majority Jammu and Buddhist-majority Ladakh.[108] It is important to note that, due to their marginalized status, non-Muslim Kashmiris are unable to check the ever-expanding political Islamic influence in the region.

Rajeev Srinivasan, another columnist for *Rediff.com,* notes in an extensive analysis that the Kashmir valley Muslim ruling class has managed to extract enormous no-strings-attached grants, totaling 10 times the state's fair share, from New Delhi: "J&K (Kashmir) is the least poor state in the country, with a rate of poverty of about 3.4 percent, compared to 26 percent for India as a whole."[109] These grants constitute economic bleeding of an impoverished India, in addition to the enormous cost of providing security in Kashmir.

The failure of successive regimes in Delhi lie in their inability to expose Kashmir valley Muslims' exaggerated portrayal of themselves as victims while marginalizing non-Muslim Kashmiris, extract unfair handouts and yet, still sponsor terror.[110]

The push towards further Islamizing Kashmir continued when the Muslim-dominated Kashmir assembly passed a bill in 2007 bringing India's only Muslim-majority state under the ambit of *sharia*.[111]

Now we move on to studying the issue of Muslim outlook in the rest of India. The Afghan Taliban's ideological underpinnings are said to have come from the Deoband Islamic seminary in present-day India. This underlines the critical importance played by this seminary in pushing Indian Muslim population ever more into radicalism. This Wahhabi-influenced Islamic institution was established in 1866, and over the years has spread a network of *madarasas* under its administrative and ideological guidance all over India. It is now the biggest Islamic institution in the country. Apparently, either through official or *hawala* (illegal or unofficial money exchange) channels, Middle East money continues to flow into India and to Islamic radicals.

Spearheading the jihadist movement in India are descendents of invaders or settlers from the Middle East, who call themselves "Muslim Indians". They are natural allies of Saudi Arabia, Pakistan and whole host of other nations trying to complete the violent "conquest" of "infidel" India for Islam.

A retired Joint-Director of Indian Intelligence Bureau notes in his book: "It is understood that the Saudi Wahhabi Sunnis and Al Azhar trained purists of Egypt have been using the Pakistani collaborators in spreading militancy amongst Indian Muslims and Muslims of South East Asia."[112]

Intense and prolonged retrogressive political preaching is bound to adversely affect the Muslim population; the "supremacy" of Islam and the privilege of being a Muslim are emphasized in sermons, while "infidel" majority Hindus are degraded. From *Where Indian Muslims Have Gone Wrong* by Aakar Patel, *Mid-day*:

> A recent poll revealed that just under 90 percent of Mumbai's Muslims, presumably the most progressive in the country, rejected a secular civil code— preferring instead *sharia* law, favoring polygamy, triple *talaq* (Muslim verbal divorce) and Islam's unequal inheritance laws which allow women half as much property as they allow men. The views of most younger and educated Muslims and of women were also the same, in almost the same proportion."[113]

The above data can be seen as representative of the Muslim outlook in all of India, as other data associated with Muslims in the rest of India are consistent with this. The preference of retrogressive *sharia* over a modern secular uniform code can be seen as associating with radical ideas at the expense of a moderate outlook.

The above poll, taken together with other information, including extremists invariably representing Muslims, appears to imply an inconvenient reality: most Indian Muslims identify with political Islam and as a result, are not moderates at all. Writing on the role of Muslim institutions in *Islamic institutions in India—Protracted Movement for Separate Muslim Identity?* Upadhyay concludes:

> Instead of providing value-based education based on modern, proper and scientific teachings to create good citizens for the overall development of Indian society, the Islamic institutions produced clergies for driving the Muslim mass to medieval era as a part of their movements for Muslim separatism.[114]

The above conclusion implies that even within secular, democratic and largely Hindu-majority India, there exist no reformed or moderate versions of Islam. This is not good news for those who insist it is possible to reform Islam any time soon.

In any case, which (non-existing) religious Muslim religious institution is going to give stamp of approval and work toward reform of Islam?

President Bush's March 2006 popular visit was almost exclusively opposed by Indian Muslims, who undercut national interests by demonstrating in favor of pan-Islamism and radicalism and by carrying posters of Osama Bin Laden.[115] There were a number of Muslim-Hindu clashes related to this visit. Anti-Bush demonstrations brought into open the diverging outlook, priorities and uneasiness of Indian Muslims' dealings with rest of the population. Here is one example: when in the 1990s hundreds of thousands of non-Muslim Indians were driven out of Kashmir by jihadis, Indian Muslim groups were busy raising funds for displaced Kosovar Muslims, while doing almost nothing to aid their fellow Indians, who were under attack by their religious compatriots.

It is illustrative to analyze views of a Muslim who was born and bred in India but was educated in the western world and who makes a living specializing in foreign affairs. One such an individual is Fareed Zakaria, the well-known author, commentator and international editor of *Newsweek.* He describes the Islam he had encountered in India growing up as "The rich, colorful, pluralistic, and easygoing Islam of my youth".[116] Yet he was oblivious to the reality that in his youthful days, in every Muslim majority area of South Asia, non-Muslims had been marginalized, were fearful and were leaving for parts of India with Hindu majority.

In an interview, Zakaria notes that "[The Indian Muslim] faces discrimination and exclusion. A good part of the problem is their lack of real political power".[47] In another interview he has taken the line on Kashmir that is often taken by the likes of hardcore Islamists, accusing India of "a military occupation of people [in Kashmir] who do not want to be occupied" and "suppressed popular movements".[117]

Given the nature of jihad waged on India, with a growing and significant support base among Indian Muslim populace and the unfortunate fate of non-Muslims in every Muslim majority area of South Asia, it would be surprising if Indian Muslims did not face discrimination and exclusion. Muslims are simply feared and distrusted in this part of the world. As discussed before, political power for Muslims in South Asia has invariably turned into state-sponsored jihad on non-Muslims. What is also notable is Zakaria's convenient neglect of non-Muslim ethnic cleansing in the Pakistani part of Kashmir and Kashmiri Muslims' widespread support for jihad directed at the Indian state, which invited the military crackdown.[110] Pakistan could simply solve the Kashmir conflict by absorbing Muslims from the Indian part of Kashmir and settling them in Pakistani part of Kashmir and in the rest of Pakistan (Pakistan should do that; after all, it kicked out most non-Muslims from the portion of Kashmir it controls and from its mainland to India).[118] But for those interested in seeing expansion of Islamic frontiers, that is an inconvenient option!

Zakaria's apparent inability to identify political Islam's influence in making Muslims conflict-prone extends to his analysis of Iraq. He blames America for the chaos in Iraq, saying "We gave them a civil war," when all America did—at an enormous cost to itself—was to try to help Iraqis build a democratic nation.[119]

Using Zakaria's terminology, given the extent of the radicalization among the Muslim populace, Muslim-sponsored terrorism in Britain could be called a "popular movement". Yet in reality, this is a jihadist movement directed at destruction of Britain, not much different from the "popular movement" in Muslim-majority Kashmir. If the British government doesn't suppress or neutralize this movement, it would put the future of Britain in jeopardy.

For all his writings on Islamic terrorism, Zakaria either doesn't understand or chooses not to understand the extent of political Islam's manipulation of Muslims and the grave danger it poses to the civilization.

The core political Islamic strategy for escalating jihad lies in falsely characterizing the Hindu majority as "oppressors" of Indian Muslims through virulent clerical sermons to create hatred of Hindus. This sets the stage for increased confrontation and separation and, eventually, dissolution of the Indian State with a fast growing Muslim population. As discussed before, with most Indian Muslims already under the influence of political Islamic ideology, the stage is set for an intensifying jihad.

The arrival of 2006 saw a quantum leap in attacks by suspected radical Islamists against majority Hindus and their religious institutions and organizations. In Assam, an Indian state bordering Islamic Bangladesh that is reeling from massive illegal influx of Bangladeshis, a Deoband-educated cleric formed a Muslim party and won many seats in local elections with an all too familiar theme—that of addressing Muslim "grievance". The United Front for Liberation of Assam, a group funded and sponsored by Islamic Bangladesh and Pakistan, has escalated attacks to drive out "Indians". This is translated to mean Hindus from rest of India, and the effort is designed to speed up the process of Islamization of the state and the Northeast region. In its latest intelligence, *Stratfor* forecasts that "New Delhi is facing a 'bleak situation' (in Indian Northeast) in which the ISI's maneuvers and Bangladesh's political troubles are sure to further constrain India's ability to dig itself out of the [Islamic] militant trap that Pakistan has set for India with the help of Bangladesh."[120]

It is not unusual for Muslim mobs to become violent after fiery Friday sermons in Indian mosques. In almost all these instances, public property, law enforcement or the majority Hindu community bear the brunt of this violence. In India's largest state, Uttar Pradesh (UP), whose Muslim population is about 20 percent of the total, clerics overwhelmingly rejected attempts in 2002 to introduce job-oriented state-financed modern education in about 20,000 *madarasas*.[121] Such a religious configuration creates and sustains a base for terror. Indeed, an Indian Intelligence official admitted in 2006 to *Newsinsight*: "[W]hat has exceptionally moved the government is that UP is becoming a big *Lashkar* (LeT) base".[122] There is widespread Indian Muslim clerical resistance to expelling illegals from Islamic Bangladesh. This resistance fits in with the idea of enhancing the Islamic thrust into India.

In a statement that shocked even officials of the state Health Department, Ahmad Hasan, the family planning minister of Uttar Pradesh, urged Muslim women to produce as many healthy children as they want, stating that the state government would give Rs 1,000 (a big sum by Indian standards) towards the care of each child.[123] What is notable is Islamists taking strategic cabinet positions to carry out their jihadist agenda; these agendas are diametrically opposite to what is needed. This is seen almost without exception in India. In Kerala, a southern India state, a Muslim party kept the education portfolio in coalition governments for decades to promote Muslim and Islamic interests almost exclusively at the expense of others. C. Issac has stated: "In all the 25 years the Muslim league followed the policy of filling up of all posts in the educational department with Muslims."[124] It is no stretch to say that one of the rare nationalist Muslims in a position of power is President Abdul Kalam, who was financially helped by Hindus in his younger days and who as a result has kept away from pan-Islamic agenda.

Radical Muslim pressure against the Indian government is intensifying. A staunch supporter of Afghan Taliban and a top Indian cleric, Shahi Imam Bukhari, representing a coalition of Indian Muslim clerics, demanded across-the-board reservations for Muslims at a meeting with Prime Minister Singh on April 18, 2006. He also issued a veiled threat: "We do not want to chart a different path, but would be forced to do so if our demands are not met".[125]

With Muslims constituting only about 15 percent of the population, in comparison to the Hindu majority's 80 percent, and due to Muslim under-representation in decision-making positions that require education, efficient and fast Islamization of India has not occurred. This has frustrated jihadis. Given their inclination toward political Islam, Indian Muslims are unlikely to embrace education wholeheartedly any time in near future; hence, a different way has to be found. If across-the-board job reservations could be enacted for Indian Muslims, including positions in military and law enforcement agencies, the goal of placing jihadist sympathizers and jihadis at positions of influence and power could be achieved.

Muslim under-representation in professional jobs is most likely due to clerical discouragement regarding modern education and joining the mainstream. Hence, instituting reservations for Muslims does nothing to address this self-induced deficiency. With Pakistan and Bangladesh already standing out as a 25 percent permanent and almost exclusive reservation of land, wealth and opportunities for Muslims and most non-Muslims already driven away from these regions and now squeezed into present day India, it is hard to justify further reservation for Indian Muslims. If any justification can be given at all, it is clearly non-Muslim Indians who need reservations in India.

Islamic radicals see proportional Muslim reservation in jobs and education as part of an integral strategy to extend Islam's boundaries. A proportional Muslim reservation, given the Muslim population growth rate of over 1.5 times the majority Hindu or non-Muslim growth rate, is indeed a convenient way of marginalizing non-Muslims in the long run.[95] Unfair reservation for Indian Muslims takes wealth away from the deserving majority and others, granting them instead to undeserving Muslims. The result is an India with an increasingly poor and illiterate majority, whose Muslim population will be wealthier, better-placed, and sympathetic to radicals. A case in point: it was noted in this section that the jihadist movement in Kashmir strengthened over the years through an unfair pseudo-reservation system in favor of Kashmir valley Muslims.

Omar Khalidi has interesting credentials for an American jihadist of Indian origin. Khalidi obtained his doctorate in 1994 from the University of Wales in Islamic studies. He is currently on staff at Agha Khan Institute at Massachusetts Institute of Technology. Khalidi is relatively unique among South Asian jihadis in that he understands the importance of Muslims obtaining political power, as well the role of modern education and occupying decision-making administrative positions in the society. While such a goal can be seen as a normal aspiration of any community activist, his one-sided portrayal and selective use of data to favor his Muslim community at the expense of others puts him in the category of a jihadist scholar. In his writings, he has consistently portrayed Indian Muslims as being victimized, attacked, and discriminated, while saying little or nothing about the ongoing jihad, which includes massive ethnic cleansing, conducted on non-Muslims in South Asia with active support from Muslims. Khalidi clearly understands the need to reach out to non-Muslim Indians and to create a feeling of guilt about the dismal state of Indian Muslims, in order to extract concessions that would eventually doom them.

Khalidi is a proponent of reconfiguring districts in many Indian states to create "compact Muslim zones" where Muslims' culture and rights could be "safeguarded". It doesn't matter to him, as some have pointed out, that India has more than safeguarded Muslim interests at a constitutional level, even at the expense of social cohesiveness and national security.[126,127] Looking at this suggestion from a jihadist angle is revealing: Khalidi is devising new ways by which Muslims can achieve political power within certain areas in a secular and democratic India.

This is a clever ploy. As pointed before, in every Muslim-majority area of South Asia, including ones within India, non-Muslims have been marginalized and ethnically cleansed in a massive way. Also, once Muslims in these regions achieve power, the regions have become jihad bases for further destabilizing India.

Khalidi published a book in 2005 titled *Muslims in Indian Economy*.[128] This book discusses the shortcomings of Muslims in India—the lack of proportional representation in government, private jobs, law enforcement agencies and armed forces, and education, as well as the prevalence of poverty and illiteracy. The blame was squarely placed on the majority Hindu community and the government. An objective analysis would have concluded otherwise: most Indian Muslim problems, including the ones under discussion, are self-inflicted. Besides, most Indian Muslims are under the spell of extremists. As India is currently being targeted by neighboring Islamic nations for conquest, and as these nations are finding ready recruits among Indian Muslims, no sane government could afford the luxury of proportional representation of Muslims in law enforcement and in the armed forces.

In the category of "other workers" listed in the 2001 Indian census report, Muslims enjoyed 49.1 percent representation, while the Hindu majority had only a 35.5 percent share. Thus, a higher percentage of Muslims are in these kinds of jobs as compared to majority Hindus. In another category of household industries workers, Muslims representation was 8.1 percent—double the national average of 4.2 percent (only 3.2 percent for majority Hindus). This implies that bulk of Muslims who drop out from schools seek gainful employment and start earning at younger age.[129,130] Another independent study, published in the *Economic Times,* found that "Hindus and Muslims are not only very close when it comes to average household income, expenditure and savings, they match each other even in terms of ownership of select consumer goods."[131]

The conclusion that follows is that Muslims in India are economically comparable to Hindus, once their reluctance to embrace modern education is taken into account.

Yet for Prime Minister Manmohan Singh's United Progressive Alliance, which was elected to power through a Muslim vote-bloc controlled by jihadis, Khalidi's book had the "ingredients" necessary to reverse the "injustice" done to Indian Muslims. Islamist interests in this regime are well-served by the presence of several Muslim cabinet ministers. The ruling regime established a committee headed by retired justice Sachar to produce a report largely based upon Khalidi's work.

Not surprisingly, the Sachar Committee, stocked with Muslims, called for a sweeping and far–reaching system of freebies allotted to Muslims, from preferred student admissions in Indian elite schools to job allotment.[132] It called for allotting an increased number of loans to Muslims and for evaluating the contents of schools texts, presumably to ensure that Muslims and Islam are portrayed in the best manner as possible and to make the unbelievers least prepared to counter jihad.

A coordinated jihadist pressure was following through. In a significant development, after the tabling of the Sachar report, Muslim parliamentarians cut across party lines to hand over a wish list of sorts. It called for establishing exclusively Muslim schools, colleges and professional institutions across the nation. In addition, the parliamentarians demanded two hundred thousand scholarships, most of which would be funded through tax collected from struggling and law-abiding non-Muslim Indians (most tax revenues come from salaried class and big business in India, staffed or owned mostly by non-Muslims).[130]

With a per capita income of just $530 dollars per year (2003), Indians are among the most impoverished people on the planet. A 2006 family health survey conducted in India found that 46 percent of its children under the age of 3 were underweight, even surpassing 28 percent for children under the age of 5 in sub-Saharan countries. Anemia, a condition reflecting malnutrition was found among 79 percent of Indian children in the 6-35 months age group, up from 74 percent only seven years ago.[133]

Nonetheless, Indian Muslim leaders decided that if free oil couldn't be found to achieve a good lifestyle and to practice free-flowing jihad, the sweat and blood of "infidels", in the form of tax-money could provide just that! That the elected Muslim leaders in India would make such an unconscionable demand shouldn't be surprising. The Islamic trilogy is very clear about this: as unbelievers, the non-Muslim Indians do not even deserve to live (Section:

Conquest by Design). In addition, clerical sermons are designed to unfairly put the blame for self-induced Muslim ills on the beleaguered majority.

Indeed, jihadis are making their intentions increasingly transparent. Indian security expert B. Raman notes in an article:

> A Delhi-based intellectual who attended the meeting convened by one of the Ministries of the Government of India to discuss the implementation of the Sachar Committee report on the condition of Muslims in India, said that at the meeting some Muslim leaders threatened that there would be more jihadi terrorism in India if the report was not implemented in toto.[134]

Having managed to market the flawed idea successfully—with no entity of influence countering the flawed analysis behind the Sachar report and Khalidi's book—that Muslims in India are facing "injustice", the die was cast. Faced with the prospect of mass demonstrations and full-fledged terrorism that would result from fiery Friday sermons all over Indian mosques, exhorting Muslims to rise up against "injustice", the Manmohan Singh's regime, propped up by jihadis, has unsurprisingly played into their hands—when this regime decided to implement all of the recommendations of the Sachar report.[135]

In summary, the Sachar Committee recommendations had the ingredients—by design—to accelerate the process of jihad in India, if implemented. This is a sophisticated form of jihad waged on an unsuspecting population!

With radicals appearing to control the Muslim voting block, and with Hindu majority votes divided, most parties are finding themselves having to placate political Islam. According to *Newsinsight.net*: "except the BJP (considered a Hindu nationalist party) terrorist links are showing up in leaders connected to several mainline parties".[122] Manmohan Singh's Congress party, which was implicated by India's own intelligence agency in being infiltrated by jihadis, took a number of steps within the past two and a half years to placate Islamists. India's anti-terrorism law, POTA, was rescinded, as it was considered "anti-Muslim".[136] The Indian Supreme Court's verdict to identify and expel illegals from Bangladesh was circumvented, as its proposal was considered too troublesome for Bengali-speaking Indian Muslims.[136] Singh seems to outdo even jihadis for the cause of political Islam when he stated in Dec. 2006: "We will have to devise innovative plans to ensure that minorities, particularly the Muslim minority, are empowered to share equitably in the fruits of development. They must have the first claim on resources".[137] Sonia Gandhi, the Congress party President and Singh's boss, went a step further. She wrote a letter as part of a 2007 election campaign in UP, specifically pleading to the Muslim clergy in the state to "help me generously to fight against caste and communalism [read majority Hindus, already targeted by jihadis] so that I can build a society of your dreams..."[138] With most clergy in UP representing political Islam, this is nothing less than promising to work for a jihad-sponsoring Islamic India!

For years now, Indian democracy has been caving into the effective Muslim vote-block politics of jihadis. Successive

Indian regimes have been unable to take steps to resettle over 300,000 Hindus driven out of the Muslim-majority Kashmir valley. A Muslim minister in UP cabinet issued a fatwa—a religious edict—to kill creators of Danish cartoons.[136] Even though this was in violation of Constitution he had sworn to uphold, no action was taken against him, presumably because he has a wide following among local Muslims. The icing on the cake was a 2005 unanimous resolution passed by Kerala's elected assembly that called for the release of Madani, jailed in a neighboring Tamilnadu prison. A proven hardcore Islamic radical and prime-accused in terrorist bombings, Madani has a large following among Kerala's 26 percent Muslim voting block.[136]

With Indian democracy under a political Islamic siege, there is a growing impression among majority Hindus that justice will not be served and their interests not protected. A low point was reached in 2002 when Hindu devotees in a train compartment were burnt alive by a Muslim mob in Godhra in Indian state of Gujarat. In the ensuing riots Hindu mobs retaliated by taking law into their own hands resulting in scores Muslims and Hindus killed.[139]

Hindu temples do not stage political sermons by religious leaders, unlike most other religions in India. The overall Hindu literacy rate is only about 60 percent and tens of millions are impoverished.[140] In the name of maintaining social harmony and due to jihadist intimidation, Indian media has avoided publishing objective analysis on political Islam. All of this has led to an unprepared nation standing as the world's worst victim of terrorism. But Indian Muslim communities suffer from no such inhibitions; political sermons are the norm in Indian mosques or *madarasas*, as are inflammatory accusations against the Hindu majority and the government.

For Indian democracy to break out of the political Islamic siege and to set the stage for an effective Indian response, the thus-far-nonchalant Hindu majority, constituting 80 percent of the population, must be mobilized. If caste divisions are thought to come in the way of Hindu mobilization, this can be dispelled with a look at the Srilankan Hindu mobilization against what were portrayed as Singhalese injustices. The success of the political Islamic strategy lies in characterizing itself as a victim even as it, arguably, victimizes India. All of this proves that creating the perception of injustice or grievance, either real or invented, is among the best ways of mobilizing a population. A campaign on political Islamic "injustices" not only has the potential to mobilize the Hindu majority population, it should also put Islamists on the defensive by discrediting their propaganda. Escalating political Islam-inspired terror acts on Hindus, the related economic bleeding, and land loss to Muslims and Muslim reservations are majority grievances.

Although there has been considerable wealth creation in recent times, thanks to burgeoning software industries and call-center positions, the poor in most Indian villages and towns have not seen a share of this wealth. This is due to expenses related to fighting political Islam and subsidizing the Muslim-majority Kashmir; these expenses take up a considerable portion of India's scarce resources. Local governments, and even private and public corporations, are also saddled with extra security-related expenses. Indeed,

India is racking up huge budget deficits—the combined 2005 state and federal budget deficit was running at 9 percent of GDP.[141]

In the Indian government's estimation, at least $150 billion is needed over the next 10 years to develop India's inadequate infrastructure.[142] Nonetheless, soon after coming to power in November 2004, Manmohan Singh announced a $5.3 billion four-year development and reconstruction package for Kashmir.[143] To put this in perspective: India's annual defense budget in 2004 dollars was about $17.5 billion.[144] The Muslim-controlled Kashmir government and legislature, with a track record of sympathy for political Islam, has a history of not using development money wisely. Also, these grants to Kashmir come at the expense of the rest of India, where most non-Muslims live. People in the rest of India, who pay most of India's taxes, need investments to improve the infrastructure for job creation.

Globalization and television penetration has left the poor in the rest of India dissatisfied with their status. Maoist or naxal ideologies have stepped in to provide an alternate vision. Perhaps only a handful understand that Maoist vision focuses not on creating new wealth, but on distributing limited wealth through the use of force. This naxal insurgency situation developing in India is similar to the one in neighboring Nepal. But Nepal, unlike India, has very little ability to create wealth on its own, as it lacks an educated population and infrastructure.

In the past, India has put down local insurgencies, such as the one in Punjab by the Sikhs. But Maoist insurgency comes at a time when political Islam is asserting itself and Kashmir Muslim insurgency continues to bleed India. According to a recent report, the Maoist insurgency covers an area where 17 percent of the population lives.[145] In words of Prime Minister Singh, from a speech delivered in April 2006: "[this insurgency is] the single biggest internal security challenge ever faced by our country".[146] The Indian government may be finally gearing up to militarily confront Maoists and their leadership. But the root causes that have created and sustained the Maoist insurgency are poverty and lack of opportunities. This cannot be addressed unless India neutralizes the uncontainable political Islamic movement within and stops the associated economic bleeding.

Unrepentant or unpunished nations, societies or groups that were either directly or indirectly involved in the 9/11, Madrid or London attacks may have backed off directly targeting the West, due to greater Western preparedness and the threat of retaliations. But with a developing and vulnerable India, there are no such inhibitions. A grim assessment of India comes from its own intelligence officials, quoted in the *Newsinsight.net* March 2006 issue: "Post-9/11, this [terrorism] shifted to the UK, and now, it is in India. India has suddenly become a most-favored destination for terrorist groups." With radical Islamist penetration and its implications worsening, an intelligence officer further admits: "'First, we are not like the United States or UK, we do not even know the full dimension of the penetration so as to be able to understand it and counter it,' said a security officer. 'But if we do not take countermeasures now, full safeguards, then we are going to have our own 9/11. We simply cannot prevent it.'"[122]

But due to political Islam's siege of India's democracy, it seems unlikely that India will undertake effective countermeasures. There are other problems. As a society, the majority community in India had been under slavery, first by Muslim invaders and later by British colonizers, for over six hundred years. Such a population doesn't nurture leadership and avoids confrontation, even as a defensive measure. It was only in the 1980s that India as a nation started competing successfully in just one area: software engineering. This competence is yet to permeate other areas, including politics and governing. Unfortunately, criminals are becoming career politicians in India. For instance, in the India state of Karnataka, 91 out of 104 candidates with criminal records— many of them violent—stood for state assembly, and 8 out of 12 for the national assembly.[147] According to a May 2007 report in the *Wall Street Journal* about 25 percent of the 535 elected members of the Indian parliament have pending criminal cases.[133]

Manmohan Singh, a unelected technocrat now posted at the most important job of Prime Minister, is known for his lack of worldview in matters of foreign policy and security matters. His own, now disgraced foreign minister Natwar Singh remarked in 2006, "I have worked with him (Manmohan Singh) for 40 years... he knew nothing of foreign affairs...".[148] Under his and Congress party's leadership, India is increasingly caving into political Islam (previous sections), even as other victim nations are strengthening their laws and resolve to fight this enemy. By Singh's own admission, terrorism is India's most dangerous threat.[149] Arguably, Singh may be India's greatest weak link. A well-respected public affairs magazine says: "Manmohan Singh is not a politician. He has no political instinct. He has no memory of the wounds inflicted on this country, though he presumably witnessed [1947] Partition as a boy. He has no political constituency."[150]

In addition to taking internal policy decisions that have led to enhancing the jihadist siege of India, Prime Minister Singh may be embarking on inadvertently enhancing the Pakistani thrust into India, by making borders between the two nations soft as part of solving the Kashmir "dispute".[151] Indian political leadership has yet to understand that accords with political leaders in Pakistan (even if they are made in good faith) are irrelevant to the de facto expansionist power in Pakistan—political Islam.

The Indian army has thus far stopped people from Pakistan, with its high population growth rate, from coming to India in search of opportunities, a country whose language, dress, and food they share. But non-Muslim Indians have no interest in looking for opportunities in an Islamic Pakistan. Making the borders soft is sure to lead to a one-way transfer of Muslim population into India, along with jihadis from Pakistan.[152] This is certain to speed up the ongoing political Islamic destruction and conquest of India.

Congress President Sonia Gandhi's inexperience and lack of credentials are also turning out to be a big handicap for a nation threatened by jihadis. The inability to talk about policy issues beyond prepared text—which Manmohan Singh and Sonia Gandhi share—is disappointing for a democracy (although not surprising). An overall literacy rate of only about 60 percent has given India a truly representative democracy, one that elects not particularly able lawmakers and leaders.

A not-unlikely scenario is one of India becoming highly destabilized; in the wake of this destabilization, the epicenter of terror and political Islam would extend from Afghanistan-Pakistan through India and connect with Bangladesh. The successful political Islamic siege of India has important lessons for the rest of the civilized world and their non-Muslim or unbeliever populations. It also shows the critical role played by Pakistan and Saudi Arabia in passionately sponsoring jihad.

Jihad Buildup

The multi-front jihad-based conquest so many non-Muslim nations are subjected to is a vision plotted and executed by external sponsors and internal nodes of political Islam—Muslim religious institutions. The first stage of this conquest involves jihad buildup, where resident Muslim populations are indoctrinated or brainwashed into shunning mainstream and embrace increasingly medieval Arab customs in the name of Islam. Once the Muslim population becomes receptive, clerics issue *fatwas* or religious injunctions—such as mandatory praying of five times a day or to stop serving "infidel" customers who use alcohol. These steps and the resulting outlook gradually alienate resident Muslims from mainstream as they fall behind in every measure of human development. Conveniently, the blame for Muslim backwardness is pinned on the non-Muslim majority or the

State—and this becomes a source of "grievance" or "injustice", and evolves into a movement for asserting "minority rights".

By analyzing data from India and its surroundings we now understand how the next phase of this jihad buildup is carried out: the nation under attack is sucked or pressurized into spending its resources first to unfairly subsidize and into allotting an unfair share of opportunities to its Muslim population and then into controlling an escalating Muslim-based violence or insurgencies. In the meantime, the Muslim population increases by leaps and bounds. Eventually, non-Muslims in this weakened State will be either expelled from regions with large Muslim concentrations or will leave due to hostile conditions. This results in an expansion of Islamic frontiers or in outright conquest!

Ideological, social, political and military preemption and disproportionate retaliations for violent jihad sponsorships are a must to prevent jihad buildup and to break the back of political Islam. This is discussed in the next chapter.

Chapter Four

Policy Response

An executive summary of previous chapters is outlined below as we prepare to draft a policy response.

State sponsorship of political Islam and jihad (Chapters One and Three):

- o The terror war is primarily a consequence of the past and continuing policies of nations that constitute the axis of jihad. Along with Saudi Arabia, Pakistan and Iran may be seen as constituting the axis; these are nations at the forefront of spreading political Islam and sponsoring worldwide jihad for Islamic conquest.
- o Political Islam is a tool for Arab expansion and conquest.
- o Al-Qaeda, Taliban and Hizbollah are either symptoms of the policies pursued or proxies of this axis.
- o The resurgence of political Islam is mostly due to Saudi funding of Muslim institutions and distribution of literature around the world that promotes an even

more extreme version of political Islam—the Wahhabi interpretation of Islam.

o Evidence exists that Saudi Arabia has knowingly funded Islamic terrorist groups involved in killings of unbelievers. This has continued even after 2001.

o Under pressure from America, Saudi Arabia has scaled down jihad directed at American interests. But it has not done so against countries such as India or even Israel.

o Saudi Arabia continues to sponsor the talibanization of Muslim majority nations such as Bangladesh and of Muslim communities around the world.

o The killings and wanton destruction of the property of unbelievers are part of a systematic effort toward achieving conquest of non-Muslim land. This is a primary vision of political Islam, and these actions constitute crimes against humanity.

o Political Islam vastly exaggerates historical Muslim accomplishments in order to instill a sense of Muslim superiority, and deliberately and often falsely depicts non-Muslims as the root cause of Muslim deprivation and shortcomings, also called "grievances" or "injustices", to divert Muslim anger and to justify waging jihad.

o In nations where political Islam is dominant, jihad-building—not nation-building—is the aspiration of the nation.

o Within the past sixty years, in every Muslim-majority area of South Asia, without exception, upon achieving power Muslims have set about expelling most non-Muslims to nearby non-Muslim areas. This data unequivocally proves the genocidal intent of political Islam and its inability to coexist with non-Muslims.

o By focusing on the symptoms and on Iraq, and failing to develop a strategy to fundamentally change or neutralize axis of jihad nations, America has wasted valuable time and resources in the war on terror.

Origin and modalities of political Islam (Chapter Two):

o The Islamic trilogy—consisting of the Koran, Hadith and Sira, are considered to constitute the complete way of life by most Muslims.

o Political Islam dominates the trilogy; this makes political Islam mainstream and its outlook remarkably similar across continents. Political Islam determines both the politics of internal governing of Muslims and the way Muslims should relate to unbelievers or non-Muslims.

o Inner political Islam has kept Muslims from progressing and being open to infusion of new ideas. By not offering a positive future for Muslims or their children, political Islam has either directly or indirectly encouraged large Muslim families.

o External political Islam commands Muslims to wage a religious war (jihad) until the entire world is Islamized. Through its emphasis of jihad, political Islam converts Muslim civilians into warriors—a state within the state. This political Islamic goal of conquest grossly violates unbelievers' inalienable right to exist and to do so unmolested.

- o Prominent Islamic theologians and scholars, since the birth of Islam, have emphasized the duty to wage jihad on unbelievers. This is by no means a minority view.
- o Jihad is a multi-front struggle, with warfare or terrorism constituting just one component. The rules of jihad are that there are almost no rules; only unbelievers are expected to adhere to the Geneva Conventions.
- o Political Islam is propagated by mainstream Islamic institutions and by mainstream clerics. Radical Islam is one component of political Islam. Political Islam establishes base for radicals among the Muslim populace and gets ordinary Muslims to sponsor radicals, extremists and jihadis.
- o The origins of Islamic scriptures, which are used to justify killings of unbelievers, deserve scrutiny. Scientific analysis utilizing information in Islam's own trilogy suggests that these scriptures are likely neither to be complete nor accurately reproduced from "God's revelations".
- o The inability of political Islam to coexist with unbelievers is traced to the scripture level.

International Order Disturbed

The esteem in which religions are held by nations and societies is such that when a threat builds in God's name, nations tend to be blindsided. Even now, the parties most affected at the hands of political Islam—America, Israel, Europe, India, Russia, the Philippines, and Thailand—are all struggling to come up with an effective policy framework without resorting to open season on Muslims. Political Islam has profoundly affected the international order. It is going to take a serious effort to restore it.

The primary purpose of a religion is to define a code of conduct for its adherents to function within the framework of a society. Hence, a religion must be capable of preaching tolerance and allowing of its adherents to acquire new knowledge, compete, and create wealth in order to survive and grow. Under normal circumstances, any religion not following these requirements will lose out to other religions or other ways of life such as agnosticism or atheism. This is the law of nature and may be seen as the basis for trusting an established religion.

The inherited oil wealth in many Islamic countries, especially in Saudi Arabia, the birthplace of Islam and the place from which political Islam calls shots though Wahhabism, has changed these requirements. This unearned wealth meant the old rules of a "good religion" no longer apply. When this free money is mixed with the idea of Islamic conquest, as emphasized in the trilogy and consistently interpreted by the Islamic scholars in subsequent centuries as a duty of Muslims, it resulted in jihad to convert the entire world to Islam. It is no stretch to say that oil wealth has empowered political Islam and has resulted in the war on terror.

The only rigid interpretation appears accepted by most Muslims is all of the useful knowledge is in the Islamic trilogy. This interpretation has several consequences: Muslims are less likely to be open to modern knowledge, and the clergy, due to their command of the Koran, are the only people qualified to interpret it and hence to guide Muslims. Since clergies do not consider progress to be among the desired objectives, Muslims, to the most part, have not progressed. Progress requires figuring out new ways of doing things and seeking out new knowledge. But such an approach contradicts the presumption that the trilogy is dominant source of all useful knowledge; this makes it unacceptable to most Muslim clergies. This has made Islamic civilization extraordinarily non-performing. The evidence is there for all to see, in the form of a lack of scientific, manufacturing, and art outputs (for instance, Egypt produces just 375 books a year as compared to 4,000 from Israel, which is one-tenth its population[153]). Since according to most clergies, there is no new useful knowledge to be acquired, they channel the energy and attention of Muslim masses into worldwide jihad—the unfinished chapter of "infidel" conquest started by Islam's founder, Mohammed.

Except for oil—an inherited wealth—contemporary Islamic civilization, to the most part, has become incapable of creating wealth. With a rapidly growing population that is sustained by modern medicine and easy food availability through technology, Islamic civilization is becoming increasingly poorer. The Human Development Index (HDI) published each year by the UN is a comparative measure of life expectancy, literacy, education and standards of living. Of the 32 countries rated "High" in 2006, not one was a Muslim-majority country. However, of the 30 countries rated "Low," 16 were Muslim countries.[154] This is despite oil wealth.

There is a tendency to underestimate jihadis and their sponsoring nations. Indeed, nations such as Saudi Arabia or Pakistan are governed poorly and their scientific and technological know-how are limited. But most of this came at the expense of focusing on Islamic history and, in particular, on jihad.[9] However, considerable creativity, conceptualization and idea development has gone into "infidel" conquest, as it has been for centuries (Chapters Two and Three). Indeed, the sophistication with which a multi-front jihad is waged on unsuspecting nations is nothing short of phenomenal.

Thanks to this passion, Muslim populations, who otherwise seem disorganized, are known to come together for the cause of jihad. This is made possible due to the ongoing jihadist activities of Muslim organizations and the day-in-and-day-out emphasis of jihad in sermons. It is no exaggeration to say that the number one activity of Muslims when acting as a community is toward the cause of jihad.

We saw how even without oil wealth, in modern times, political Islam has marginalized non-Muslims in South Asia (Chapter Three). Increasingly, Muslim civilians are being indoctrinated to become foot-soldiers for jihad, and Muslim communities have been influenced to act as support and recruitment bases. We now understand who does that; it is mainstream mosques and their clerics who play the dominant and most influential role behind political Islam. This is enhanced by the resources coming from many oil-rich nations, notably Saudi Arabia and Iran.

American policy response, in recent times, has become too predictable and has operated within the confines of very restrictive rules of engagement. The exhausting and failing American involvement in Iraq has weakened the American military and has exposed the limits of its power. The Bush administration, the regime behind the Iraq occupation policy, stands discredited and finds itself short on political capital.

The enemy knows the parameters within which a weakened America now responds to threats. Still, its enemies do not obey any rules when it comes to dealing with America. jihadis claim, being part of or associated with much weaker nations, that they can't afford to play by international rules, which they claim were set by America. In other words, jihadis dictate the terms on which the terror war is conducted. This is among the primary reasons that America is making little headway in a very expensive and asymmetric war.

Political Islam's resurgence, and its adverse impact even in secular democracies, have raised inconvenient questions about what a religion is, as opposed to a political or imperialistic ideology masquerading as a religion. In this context, there is also a question of what is meant by religious freedom as defined in Universal Declaration of Human Rights and adopted and proclaimed by United Nations General Assembly resolution 217 A (III) of 10 December 1948.[155]

Saudi-funded or -trained Imams have propagated political and terror-sponsoring Wahhabi Islam all over the world, including in American prisons, on the grounds of religious freedom (the Saudi state doesn't even allow Bible to be brought onto its soil). It is unlikely that those who drafted the Universal Rights foresaw religions becoming a destabilizing force on an international scale. Classifying any version of political Islam, including Wahhabi ideology, strictly as religion, especially after 9/11 attacks, should be considered unwise. Yet federal institutions such as the State Department's Human Rights and Religious Freedom section and United States Commission on International Religious Freedom may be doing just that. The Congressional mandate issued to these federal entities to view religious freedom in the context of the obviously outdated Universal Declaration of Humans Rights needs to be revisited.

Reform of Islam and its Institutions

At a discussion with the *Washington Post* editorial board in December 2006, Secretary Rice talked of the struggle inside Islam to define the role for politics and religion. She was of the opinion that this struggle is between extremism and moderation. However, from this book's point of view, there is little evidence to support this view.

On the contrary, with political Islam dominating the scene, the struggle inside Islam is among different shades of extremism. This distinction is important in making policy initiatives.

Under what conditions does a religion reform? Historically and for good reasons, religious institutions—not individuals—carry out reforms. For reform to take place, the following condition must exist: schools of alternate or moderate religious thoughts must flourish in an institutionalized way. Such conditions must involve tolerance for alternate views, and the doctrine itself should be amenable to reform. The Islamic doctrine, defined through the trilogy, is dominated by political component and jihad (Chapter Two). How can this political component be deemphasized in order for reform to take place? Also, who will do the reforming? Hence, it may not be particularly relevant to talk about the role of moderate Muslims in initiating reform in Islam. Here is another damning, but a legitimate possibility: if political Islam is designed for conquest (Chapter Two), why should it be amenable to reform?

This raises the question of what a moderate form of Islam might look like. A moderate form of Islam would view Saudi Arabian Wahhabi Islam as the antithesis of moderation—as a fascist form of Islam. Here is the crux of the problem: most prominent Sunni mosques around the world have been generously funded by Saudi Wahhabis or by Iranian Ayatollahs on the Shiite side. A moderate mosque not only has to find its own funding, but it has to go against the Muslim "mainstream".

With Wahhabism yet to be singled out before 2001, even in America, where the Muslim population is well-educated, one would be hard-pressed to find moderate mosques. An April 2001 survey by the Council on American-Islamic Relations found 69 percent of Muslims in America saying it is "absolutely fundamental" or "very important" to have Salafi (similar to Wahhabi) teachings at their mosques (67 percent of respondents also expressed agreement with the statement "America is an immoral, corrupt society").[156] These statistics are also an indication of political Islam's influence on Muslims. Based upon these statistics, it would be reasonable to conclude that roughly 65 percent of American Muslims identified with political Islam over the American system of liberty and tolerance.

A revealing statistic from the world's largest democracy was discussed in the section *Siege of India*.[113] It shows an overwhelming majority of Indian Muslims, in a secular democratic nation with a non-Muslim majority, identifying with the extremist views of political Islam.

For Muslim scholars, brought up under the influence of exaggerated claims of glory of Islamic civilization, it is difficult to admit that Islam needs reform or that it may be fundamentally not amenable to reform (given its conquest-oriented dominance, as outlined in Chapter Two). Fareed Zakaria writes: "the key is not religious reform, but political and economic reform. The entire emphasis on a transformation of Islam is misplaced".[157] Reza Aslan claims that Islam is undergoing reformation.[158]

The example of how India and Pakistan, sharing similar culture, language and food habits but differing on religion, went divergent ways (Chapters One and Three) shows that the emphasis on religious reform is perhaps more important than other reforms. Saudi money was not even in the pipeline when Pakistan began its descent into jihad, which occurred immediately after it was partitioned from British India in 1947.

Historically, with every religion, reformation is always accompanied by the loosening of the grip that religious heads and their institutions hold over the masses. But in Islam in the last thirty-plus-years, clergy control seems to have only gone up, with funding and books for mosques coming from Wahhabi-intensive Saudi Arabia. This is accompanied by other indicators of consolidation of political Islam: the spreading of *sharia* courts, from Saudi Arabia to Iran, Pakistan, Sudan, India, Nigeria and Somalia, and unofficial ones in England. It is important to note that Al-Qaeda is a movement and that this movement has a wide-spread ideological following in the Muslim world. All of this data is telling us an inconvenient truth: increasingly, retrogressive forces are taking over Islam—this is no reformation!

This reality is not lost on some scholars. In an op-ed titled *A More Islamic Islam* Geneive Abdo points out:

The self-proclaimed secularists represent only a small minority of Muslims. The views among religious Muslims from CAIR (Council on American-Islamic Relations) more closely reflect the views of the majority, not only in the United States but worldwide (CAIR denounced any notion of a reformation as another attempt by the West to impose its history and philosophy on the Islamic world).

Consider the facts: Islamic revivalism has spread across the globe in the past 30 years, from the Middle East to parts of Africa. In Egypt, it is hard to find a woman on the street who does not wear a headscarf. Islamic political groups and movements are on the rise—from Hizbollah in Lebanon, to Hamas in the Gaza Strip and West Bank, to the Muslim Brotherhood in Egypt. Even in the United States, more and more American Muslims, particularly the young, are embracing Islam and religious symbolism in ways that their more secular, immigrant parents did not.

Similarly, the political future of the Arab world is likely to consist of Islamic parties that are far less tolerant of what has historically been the U.S. foreign policy agenda in the region and that domestically are far more committed to implementing *sharia* law in varying degrees.

In Europe and the United States, where Muslims have maximum exposure to Western culture, they are increasingly embracing Islamic values. In Britain, a growing number of Muslims advocate creating a court system based upon Islamic principles.

What all this means is that Western hopes for full integration by Muslims in the West are unlikely to be realized, and that the future of the Islamic world will be much more Islamic than Western.[159]

Right to Exist

The inability of political Islam to coexist raises deep risk-management issues regarding unbeliever survival. Political Islam, regardless of where it is practiced, follows one set of texts—the Islamic trilogy—and this is the reason for remarkable similarity in practice across continents. Also, as discussed earlier, the lack of any reputed Muslim religious institution that offers alternate and moderate versions of Islam is notable. Political Islam is self-perpetuated by high Muslim population growth rates, even in nations where Muslims are a minority. Hence, it is no stretch to conclude the following: non-Muslims have no future, as the resident Muslim population grows to reach majority status (see the data on South Asia in the previous chapter). This is a genocidal threat.

Along with the rise in Muslim population, instabilities will also escalate well before Muslim majority is reached. This has no parallel with any other religion. This is what distinguishes political Islam from other religions. An effective policy response should not only address the terror threats of the immediate tomorrow but should also address the much more serious strategic issue, the unbelievers' right to exist in the long run and to preemptively put forth policy measures to ensure their secure existence. In other words, preemption is a must.

Even if certain mainstream Islamic institutions appear to practice moderation, given political Islam's track record, there is every reason to believe that these institutions will resort to more open and aggressive jihad once their power base increases. Hence, policy response should be designed to neutralize Muslim organizations that represent political Islam in any way or form, on the grounds of right of preemption. This includes even those that do not appear to be threatening at this time.

Here is a situation described in British mosques, reported in 2006, with Saudis again playing the primary role in sponsoring jihad abroad:

> A *Dispatches* reporter attends mosques run by organizations whose public faces are presented as moderate and finds (Muslim) preachers condemning integration into British society, condemning democracy and praising the Taliban for killing British soldiers...
>
> Dispatches has investigated a number of mosques run by high profile national organizations that claim to be dedicated to moderation and dialogue with other faiths. But an undercover reporter joined worshippers to find a message of religious bigotry and extremism being preached. He captures chilling sermons in which Saudi-trained preachers proclaim the supremacy of Islam, preach hatred for non-Muslims and for Muslims who do not follow their extreme

beliefs - and predict a coming jihad. "An army of Muslims will arise," announces one preacher. Another preacher said British Muslims must "dismantle" British democracy - they must "live like a state within a state" until they are "strong enough to take over." The investigation reveals that the influence of Saudi Arabian Islam, Wahhabism, extends beyond the walls of some mosques to influential organizations that advise the British government on inter-community relations and prevention of terrorism. The investigation reveals Saudi Arabian universities are recruiting young Western Muslims to train them in their extreme theology, then sending them back to the West to spread the word. And the Dispatches reporter discovers that British Muslims can ask for *fatwas*, religious rulings, direct from the top religious leader in Saudi Arabia, the Grand Mufti.[160]

Consider the scenario of aliens visiting Earth. If the evidence gradually develops that the alien intends to exterminate humans, this alien-human conflict becomes a death-fight. Without either driving out the aliens or destroying them, humans have no future. In such a situation, if time is not on their side, humans have to hit back swiftly and decisively. A human retaliation may lead to the destruction of the entire alien civilization, including alien non-combatants.

In his book Jackson Nyamuya Maogoto examines legitimate use of force in counteracting state-sponsored terrorism. After examining the issues in the context of International Chief Justice jurisprudence and UN resolutions, he points out: "The prohibition on the use of force has been traditionally balanced against the 'inherent' right to self-defense as contained in the UN charter" and importantly, he notes on the evolution of retaliatory defense, "It will be submitted that the UN charter regime on the use of force (on the states sponsoring terror) is visibly engaged in the process of change, especially in light of the September 11 attacks."[161] Conclusion: a victim nation of terror is left to decide how best it can retaliate to the unconventional terror war imposed in the name of Islam.

A proportionate response to acts of jihad has proven to be ineffective and very costly. Instead of reducing the threat, it has emboldened political Islam and increased its power base among its adherents.

When an enemy is proven in his intent to annihilate us, the ethics of warfare allow a response designed to comprehensively remove the enemy's ability to exterminate us. This should naturally mean a disproportionate response. A disproportionate response at times may lead to high civilian casualties, as political Islam has set up base among indoctrinated and largely sympathetic Muslim civilians.

Reform of Islam appears unlikely in the near future. As part of a robust risk management policy and civic responsibility, the time may have come to ask whether non-Muslim states should initiate policy measures that will break the back of political Islam, so that their Muslim residents may be liberated to alternate faiths or way of life.

Think Political Islam

By now, it must be clear that the unbelievers are at war with political Islam, not just with radical Islam. This necessary paradigm shift must be understood in going forward. This approach still doesn't call for war on most Muslims. After all, Muslim civilians too are victims of political Islam. Political Islam's basis is in the trilogy and is identified with mainstream mosques and *madarasas*—Muslim religious schools. In most Muslim-majority nations, political Islam determines the dynamics of a nation's outlook towards itself and outsiders. As a rule, this outlook is destabilizing and is geared towards conquest of unbelievers through jihad.

As it has been discussed in first Chapter, America as a whole, both liberals and conservatives, have not understood the new political Islamic enemy well. On the right, President Bush's consistent emphasis of Islam as a "religion of peace" in the early part of presidency couldn't have been helpful to the war on terror, although he did stop using this phrase in his second term and began to use the phrases "Islamic fascism" and "Islamic fascists" more frequently.[162]

The nature of the war itself, which has been groups or actors that are unofficially patronized by states with global reach and influence but that obey no rules of engagement, has created tricky policy options. A clarification is in order here: although Al-Qaeda was not officially patronized by states such as Saudi Arabia or Pakistan, there have been reports of it receiving assistance from sympathetic government officials (for instance, through Pakistan's ISI) and non-governmental organizations linked to these governments (Chapter One). What this shows is the power and influence of political Islam, in defiance of policies set up by top national leaders. In the book *Frontline Pakistan: The Struggle With Militant Islam,* Zahid Hussein mentions that the Pakistani President Gen. Pervez Musharraf is in an impossible position due to jihadi penetration of Pakistan's army and intelligence.[163] Hence, relying on governments in Islamic nations such as Pakistan or Saudi Arabia where political Islam is the overriding power is no way to win the war.

Ahmed Rashid, a noted Pakistani author and journalist, mentions the dilemma faced by leaders such as Musharraf as a ruler of nations dominated by political Islam: "In the rapidly unfolding crisis in Pakistan, no matter what happens to President Pervez Musharraf—whether he survives politically or not—he is a lame duck. He is unable to rein in Talibanization in Pakistan or to guide the country toward a more democratic future."[164]

With regard to political Islam, America faces three types of enemies: quasi-independent groups such as Al-Qaeda, openly antagonistic ones such as Iran, and superficial allies such as Pakistan or Saudi Arabia. America is still powerful enough to deal with the first kind, but given the damage done to American military and the lack of political capital, America will find it hard to confront Iran militarily all by itself. A weakened America has little leverage in dealing with Pakistan or Saudi Arabia. Increasingly emboldened, for these nations, it is slowly and yet surely a trip back to the return of old habits—sponsoring worldwide jihad. However, by going after the theological and ideological foundations of political Islam, America can weaken them all.

In this new war, the enemy builds up military strength in a non-Muslim state through indoctrination, infiltration from Islamic lands, and a high population growth rate of Muslim minorities under political Islamic control. The next step involves laying down a siege of the nation, and, finally, a Muslim insurgency. This multi-front tactic drains the resources away through an escalating jihad. Political Islam's siege of India tells us how this is carried out (Chapter Three). The victim nation faces poverty, expulsions of non-Muslims from Muslim majority areas, and eventually shrinkage and destruction.

Through indoctrination, political Islam prepares Islamic populations to wage a war of genocide on unsuspecting unbelievers. The Geneva Convention did not foresee this kind of warfare, and victim nations may doom themselves responding to this war strictly according to the political-Islamic interpretation of internationally accepted rules of engagement. Fundamentally, the success of the war on terror comes down to nations' willingness to adapt their strategies.

Political Islam's power structure is commanded by clerics, and their violent domineering influence has thus far prevented the trilogy from being put under microscope. This is in sharp contrast with other world religions, which have gone through introspection by the faithful and have evolved with the times.

The simplicity and strength of political Islamic ideology lies in its claims of associating all useful information and a complete way of life through the trilogy of Islam. This simplicity means there can now be well-defined ideological and physical targets associated with political Islam. Seen in a different context this simplicity can also be construed as political Islam's greatest weakness.

The core ideological strength of Western societies is their understanding of nature—called science—and common sense derived from it. The essence of the West's ideology is the reality of the modern world in which we live, while political Islam's ideology is make-believe and is therefore incapable of standing up to scrutiny (Chapter Two, Section: *Science to the Rescue*). This book differs from Mark Steyn's view: "Islamism is militarily weak but ideologically confident. The West is militarily strong but ideologically insecure".[165]

Progress is achieved by manipulating nature, by using tools called science and engineering. The largely atheist Chinese and non-Christian Hindus in India are achieving progress by embracing this modern ideological vision, which was first developed in the West. For instance, common sense tells us that the technology existing at the time of Islam's founder Mohammed was not robust enough to reproduce "God's revelations" accurately. It is this modern vision that is capable of discrediting political Islam (Chapter Two). But to execute this strategy as part of a policy response, Western societies must graduate from political correctness to political smartness.

With war on terror dominating the Federal Government's bureaucracy, it should be immensely useful to make it mandatory for all federal employees to undertake a short course on political Islam. Even the State Department's policies appear to be inadvertently aiding political Islam, at the expense of its victims.[166] Without this mandatory course, even federal executives could get stuck in outdated views and undermine the war effort.

Radical Islam could be kept in check through repressive policies, as is the case in Hosni Mubarak's Egypt or in Saddam Hussein's Iraq. But political Islam, mostly left untouched by this repression, will continue to destabilize a nation, eventually putting it in a no-win situation.

A leader of a Muslim-majority nation or a community could be opposed to radical Islam, but unlikely to take a firm stand against political Islam, because political Islam represents the mainstream. But without neutralizing political Islam, it is not possible to neutralize radical Islam. In other words, political Islam is the swamp that creates and sustains mosquitoes (Muslim radicals, extremists and jihadis).

The American policy of working with "moderate" Saudi leadership, or with Musharraf in Pakistan, falls in this category. These relationships may have led to reduction of jihad directed at the West. But Pakistan and Saudi Arabia have continued jihad directed at Israel, India, and others. With political Islam as their guiding influence, these societies have changed little since 2001. The educational reforms carried out in these nations, at behest of America, do almost nothing to discredit political Islam, because this requires alternate articulation and questioning of political Islamic doctrines and scriptures at the theological level—a very explosive proposition, and an impossible one for the ruling class. Under the current circumstances, as well as in the near future, no Muslim leader can be expected to do that. Therefore, only an outside non-Muslim power with ideological, military, technological and economic clout can do this job.

A great deal of resource and effort has gone into the so-called public diplomacy aimed towards reducing "Muslim

Street's" anger towards America. This has involved taking Muslim students to World Cup games in Germany, hosting training seminars for Arab journalists or Under Secretary of State Karen Hughes talking to Muslim women around the world.[167] Unfortunately, none of these initiatives drive a much-needed wedge between political Islam (the instigator behind the Street's anger) and its followers.

America and Western Europe have had considerable success and experience as non-occupying powers when they discredited and eventually defeated Soviet communism. First, Soviet Communism failed to bring progress to the people it ruled. But what made it collapse was when the United States informed the people of the Eastern Bloc why their system did not work and showed them alternatives that did: namely, the democracy and freedom embodied in America and in most Western nations. In the end it is this realization—not Western occupation—that led to the revolution from within.

As discussed in Chapter One, American occupation succeeded both in Germany and Japan because their strongest institutions were weakened and discredited by the defeat. However, when America entered Iraq, it inadvertently created an opening for the leading adversarial power— political Islam—to flourish; as a result, America became trapped there. In Afghanistan, radical Islam was considerably weakened by Taliban and Al-Qaeda defeat in the hands of America and its allies, but political Islam in Afghanistan, the leading adversarial power behind radical Islam, was left intact. But as an occupying power in need of local cooperation, America can in no way afford to discredit political Islam. The conclusion follows: as an occupying power and a former adversary, America is not well-positioned to liberate Iraq or Afghanistan from political Islam. America's best chances of weakening political Islam and to achieve true liberation, as it did with former Soviet Union, is as a non-occupying power.

During the Cold War, Communism was largely seen as a front for advancing the imperialist ambitions of the former Soviet Union. Political Islam can rightly be seen as a front for Saudi Arabian conquest. This angle opens up the possibility of liberating followers of political Islam by putting policy initiatives in place.

After all, two thousand years ago there were no followers of political Islam.

Nodes of Social Network

David Kilcullen has pointed out in an essay the importance of social network in spawning insurgencies (jihad is a form of insurgency).[168] In this book we explore these ideas further. The entities holding a network together and allowing it to grow are known as nodes. In the context of political Islam or jihad, these nodes are typically mosques, *madarasas*, Muslim organizations, associations, or any platform that brings Muslims together as a community to work on a political Islamic agenda.

As the jihad buildup intensifies, mainstream mosques become the core nodes. By now Muslim communities are under the full control of political Islam, and are indoctrinated toward jihad. Jagmohan describes in his book the role played by mosques in Kashmir:

Besides subverting almost all the organs of the State power structure, establishing complete control over the local press, and setting in motion vast propaganda machine of their own, the subversives used mosques extensively for rearing, nursing and fanning their activities... From the mosques, fitted with numerous powerful loudspeakers, came the exhortations, slogans, declarations, announcements and programs... The religious functions held in the mosques were fully exploited and the masses indoctrinated in the name of Islam and freedom. In the event of death of any "freedom fighter", special funeral prayers were held in big mosques and the occasion was used to make inflammatory speeches to whip up mass hysteria.[169]

The onset of violent jihad in Muslim-majority Southern Thailand shows how these nodes can create and sustain a violent jihadist outlook among the Muslim populace. This is usually the first step towards a full-blown Muslim insurgency with identifiable leadership(s) and a dedicated cadre. From Raman:

[In southern Thailand] Targeted attacks with small arms and ammunition on individuals with extreme cruelty, multiple explosions with minimum casualties and attacks on places considered anti-Islam, such as places of entertainment, continue to be reported almost every day. The individuals targeted are not only Buddhists, but also public servants, including Muslims, viewed as collaborators of the Government... Unidentifiable jihadi forces orchestrated by an invisible command and control have been keeping the security forces at bay... the jihadi leaders are neither visible nor audible. No recorded messages, no statements, no intercepts, no human intelligence derived either from sources or during the interrogation of arrested suspects. There are hardly any arrests—not even accidental.[170]

The lack of scientific and engineering output from Islamic civilizations is an indication that Muslim populations are not particularly well-organized, except when they work under auspices of the nodes to wage jihad. This shows that for political Islam to mobilize and fight back, it must overwhelmingly rely on these nodes. This major weakness must be exploited. The nodes can be weakened. Nodes get their ideological standing from theology; their financial and logistical sponsorship is predominantly from axis of jihad nations.

The enemy nodes of social network, which were off limits previously due to a lack of knowing the enemy and restrictive rules of engagement, are now ready for ideological, political, military, economic, and social assault on the basis of right of preemption. In this chapter, ideas are presented on discrediting the standing of the nodes, shutting them down if need be, and going after the backer nations of nodes. This way of waging war works to America's and other victim nations' advantage and exploits the enemy's vulnerabilities.

This book points out the lack of moderation at the Islamic institutional or nodal level. This means that policy measures can be taken at the nodal level without directly discriminating against individual Muslims. This may be the key to winning the war on terror without whole scale changes to the practice of liberty. This book envisions use of force, but only sparingly, and in a devastating and focused manner.

The first priority is to address the issue of American military deployment in Iraq and Afghanistan.

Direction Change

I state now what is obvious: the people of Iraq or Afghanistan are under the influence of political Islam, and hence they are not ready for nation-building or democracy; for that matter, they are not ready to listen to America (Chapter One). Increasing troop strengths in Iraq, as part of a "surge" put forward by President Bush in January 2007, is clearly not going to work.[171] The question of whether America needs to cut its losses and get out of both Iraq and Afghanistan as soon as possible is quite an appropriate one. As is pointed out in the excerpts below, America is not ready for the kind of rules engagement that it would take to stabilize Iraq or even Afghanistan.

Edward Luttwak points out in a decisive analysis titled *Dead End: Counterinsurgency Warfare as Military Malpractice*:

All its best methods, all its clever tactics, all the treasure and blood that the United States has been willing to expend, cannot overcome the crippling ambivalence of occupiers who refuse to govern, and their principled and inevitable refusal to out-terrorize the insurgents, the necessary and sufficient condition of a tranquil occupation.[40]

If out-terrorizing is what it takes to stabilize Iraq, America will have to do a Saddam on Iraq—an unlikely proposition! Even then, these steps will do little to neutralize political Islam and therefore will not aid in reaching the ultimate goal: a functional democracy in Iraq.

Indeed, the overall tide is going against America. The Iraq Study Group has also reached the conclusion that America should pull out of Iraq.[172] But several knowledgeable observers have voiced reservations about many of the Group's recommendations. For instance, its suggestion that America work with Iran and Syria to stabilize Iraq may be a non-starter, due to strategic and important ideological divergences with the U.S. globally and in Iraq. Likewise, the suggestion of increasing the number of American advisors with Iraqi army while withdrawing significant proportion of American troops would mean these advisors would be left with little protection. Based upon the background of the people comprising the Study Group, there is little to suggest that the Group understands how political Islam operates. This fundamentally limits the Group's utility.

Carl Ponatta points out the increasing anti-Americanism in Iraq:

Most disturbing, support among Iraqis for attacks on coalition forces registered at 61 percent in the September 2006 poll—up from 47 percent in January 2006. Among Shia, support for attacks is 62 percent; among Sunnis, 92 percent. A September 2006 poll for the Defense Department found somewhat lower levels of support for the attacks, but still quite disturbing: 75 percent of Sunnis supported them – up from 14 percent in 2003. An October 2006 poll by the British Ministry of Defense found similar results. And a January 2005 poll by Zogby International found that 53 percent of Sunnis supported attacks on U.S. troops at that time... Generally speaking, Iraqi sentiments regarding the U.S. presence have grown steadily more negative since the summer of 2003... 79 percent of Iraqis say that the United States is having a negative influence on the situation in Iraq, with just 14 percent saying that it is having a positive influence.[173]

Without order achieved through effective law enforcement, American efforts to stabilize Iraq simply can't succeed. One keeps hearing from both Iraq and Afghanistan that the local law enforcement is not yet ready to deal effectively with insurgents. Nevertheless, often times in the past overly simplistic estimates had been given by the Bush administration officials as to when these forces might be ready, which were revised when the time expired. Among the future redeployment possibilities mentioned is a stronger American commitment to training Iraqis. A word of caution is needed here: The continued preaching of hatred against America across Iraqi mosques has undercut America in the eyes of Iraqis. On top of this, if America is seen as calling shots, it is hard to see how Iraqi forces will fight hard against insurgents backed by political Islam. Besides, new recruits of the Iraqi army and police are already fractured along ethnic lines. The apparent enthusiasm for enrolling into Iraqi police or military is probably a reflection of high unemployment rates and shouldn't necessarily be construed as a desire for nation-building.

Clerics and mosques are playing the roll of spoilers in Iraq since the 2003 American invasion.[40] This is further evidence that political Islam has undermined American efforts to bring democracy there.

Being under the influence of political Islam means at least a dislike, if not a downright hatred of America. The exception would be the Kurds; a bare majority of them, due to strategic compulsions, have embraced a pro-American stance. Even if some American forces are kept in friendly Iraqi Kurdish areas to protect Kurds from Turkey, it may not come as a surprise if the governing Islamic party in Turkey encourages Iraqi Sunnis, Shiites or even Al-Qaeda to go after American troops in order to clear the way for Turkey's intervention in Kurdish areas.

The Bush administration officials have claimed that by fighting Al-Qaeda in Iraq and Afghanistan, they have prevented it from going elsewhere—including America—to fight the unbelievers. But with jihadi recruitment unlikely to taper down, under the current scenario, this strategy has put America and its military in a no-win situation. In fact, these deployments are destroying the American military. This book takes the view that American reluctance to leave Iraq could be due to a lack of comprehensive policy on how to successfully execute the war on terror. An American establishment that identifies political Islam and its sponsors, recognizes the axis of jihad as the real enemy, and knows how to deal with them may be willing to expedite a quick redeployment from Iraq.

More than three years into the Iraq war, America is now confronted with the reality of finding itself in the middle of a Sunni-Shia conflict. Among the issues is the question of how this conflict will shape the dynamics of the struggle within Iraq and beyond, as well as its impact on the war on terror itself. Already there are reports of private Saudis funneling cash to Sunni Iraqi insurgents.[174] According to news reports, Saudis told Vice-President Cheney toward late 2006 of their intention to come to the aid of Sunnis in Iraq.[175] With Iran siding with the Shiite majority, the Iraqi insurgency has already blossomed into a Sunni-Shiite conflict. Considerable resources and energy from Saudi Arabia and Iran will get pulled into this inter-Muslim warfare, which would have otherwise gone into jihad directed at unbelievers. This may not be a bad thing!

The first order of priority is to make the best out of the strategic necessity of leaving Iraq. American military engagement in Iraq is a large one, involving well over 100,000 troops. Supplying and sustaining this military deployment has been taxing even for a resourceful nation. In order to supply the main divisions in and around Baghdad, the lines of communication traverse about 400 miles of hostile, insurgent-infested territory from Kuwait. This extended stay has drained American troops emotionally and psychologically, and unfortunately there is little to show for it. The sights of welcoming Iraqis and nation-building fast gave way to a hostile Iraqi public and a full-fledged insurgency for whom America troops are a favorite target. With a casualty figure now exceeding 3,000 dead and many times more injured, the American military is hurting.

Starved of cash due to a very expensive war, the American military hasn't been able to replenish its hardware adequately. New purchases are either put on hold or drastically scaled down. The Pentagon's own reports have questioned American ability to simultaneously deploy a large contingent of U.S. armed forces while America is still engaged militarily in Iraq. Gen. Barry McCaffrey, a retired U.S. Army four-star general, told *Time* magazine in January 2005, "The Army's wheels are going to come off in the next 24 months... We are now in a period of considerable strategic peril."[176] A redeployment of the American military away from battle zones in Iraq should lead to a much-needed healing and an opportunity for rebuilding the American war machine.

The situation is also turning to the worse in Afghanistan. Pakistanis are attempting to wash their hands of the Taliban infiltration from tribal North Waziristan, claiming that they have little control over this region despite repeated supposed attempts to assert such control through political and military means. Pakistan has cut a "peace" deal with a Taliban advisory council in 2005.[177] Since then, in violation of this agreement, Taliban infiltration into Afghanistan has increased several fold, making American attempts to stabilize Afghanistan untenable.

Had the tribes belonged to a different faith, it is unlikely that they would have waged a religious war against the United States. Indeed, political Islam is commanding these people to wage jihad. This again points to the reality that the United States has no other alternative but to take on political Islam as a non-occupying power. This book differs with Peter Bergen's assessment that "there should be a military, diplomatic and reconstruction "surge" to Afghanistan, a country where such efforts have a fighting chance of real success."[17]

In case of an American pullout, airpower could help to keep radical Islamists in check both in Iraq and Afghanistan. Given the nature of sectarian warfare, turning Iraq into a powerful terror base for Al-Qaeda or a radical Shia group wouldn't be easy. In the case of Afghanistan, Pakistan and Saudi Arabia will be hard-pressed to repeat the level of sponsorship they gave before 2001.

Like it did recently in Somalia and earlier in Taliban-controlled Afghanistan, the American military can be utilized without occupation to disrupt and destroy jihadis groups and discourage them from using weak nations or sympathetic ones as staging posts for jihad directed at America and its allies.

Should America pull out, a long drawn-out and intensifying conflict between Sunnis and Shiites in Iraq will eventually destabilize the region. But that is likely going to take several years. If America can implement a strategy of discrediting political Islam and go after axis of jihad nations in the meantime, it can pull the rug out from under both Sunni and Shiite versions of political Islam, which are already fighting with each other in Iraq and trying to influence events in Iraq and Lebanon.

It is understandable for America to work with the Saudis to curtail Iranian influence in Lebanon, but it must refrain from the temptation of aligning with quasi-independent Sunni extremists to contain Iran. The big picture, which is the need to neutralize political Islam both in Iran and in Saudi Arabia, shouldn't be missed.

The first and foremost responsibility of America is towards its citizens and allies who are victimized by political Islam. Short-term hardship brought to Iraqis or Afghans in the event of an American pullout, while regrettable, is not entirely the fault of the United States. Furthermore, it can be argued that the intensifying sectarian warfare in Iraq or the Taliban infiltration from sanctuaries in Pakistan have their roots in political Islam. By redirecting the war on terror and breaking the back of political Islamic movement worldwide, America can bring about the best gift for all—the gift of long-term peace, development and stability.

Grievance-based Mobilizing

Anger and hatred are mechanisms that get humans to come together to fight an enemy even at the cost of personal suffering. High priests of political Islam only know this too well. While the theological underpinnings of political Islam are used to justify terrorism directed at unbelievers, various Islamic "causes" or "grievances", often exaggerated or unjustified, have been created by Islamists to rally Muslim masses around the world. They range from pan-Islamic issues, such as the Israel-Palestinian conflict (due to the involvement of Jews and Mohammed's descendents, the Arabs, this conflict has a pan-Islamic flavor to it), to regional ones, such as the Kashmir conflict. These grievances are brought down to a personal level for the Muslim masses and lead to a buildup of anger and hatred against global or local "oppressors". However, because mosques and clerics form the core of the social network around which Muslim communities function, Muslim communities are easily pulled into jihad. Saudi funding of mosques around the world can be seen as investments in the nodes of social network, aimed at arming it with ideology and resource in order to build up grievances that will help to mobilize Muslims for jihad.

It is not necessary for a population to be particularly religious or belong just to one religion to identify with a cause and to embrace violence as a means of getting back at its perceived enemies. Although Tamil Tigers in Srilanka get their recruits mostly from the secular Hindu community, there is also a strong Tamil Christian component. In this case, Tamils had long felt that the majority Singhalese discriminated against them by taking away opportunities unfairly and giving their language second-class treatment. In other words, personalizing grievance led to community mobilizing.

Political Islam, particularly the axis of jihad, has caused immense physical and material sufferings to nations, communities and individuals around the world (Chapters One and Three). This constitutes a grievance. For instance, Americans have their own grievances against Saudi Arabia and Pakistan, which were the primary sponsors of the entities (such as Al-Qaeda or the Afghan Taliban) responsible for the 9/11 attacks. Indians have their own; so do Israelis and countless other nations.

The key towards mobilizing victimized non-Muslim populations is to develop a personal sense of grievance towards Saudi Arabia and other Islamic states that sponsor terror. Millions have seen their wealth shrink due to instabilities created by 9/11 attacks; the cost of borrowing has increased at the individual level due to the budget deficits, which have been hastened by financing expensive terror wars; infrastructure and Research and Development (R&D) are not funded adequately due to the high cost of fighting terror, and the result is a less competitive America. Millions of people in impoverished India are seeing their future evaporate due to extensive economic and social bleeding caused by Pakistan, Saudi Arabia, and many other Islamic nations. It is no exaggeration to say that Saudi Arabia and other jihad-sponsors have hit the pocketbooks of hundreds of millions of non-Muslims, thus compromising their future.

Billions of angry non-Muslims and a strong desire on the part of their nations to hold Saudi Arabia, Iran, and Pakistan accountable for acts of terror should be a significant step toward winning the war on terror.

Among the desired booklets is *Unbeliever Grievance List: Saudi Sponsorship of Unbeliever Atrocities*. This can be a powerful tool. There is a precedent: among the most important mobilizing documents produced in American history is Thomas Jefferson's *Declaration of the Causes and Necessity for Taking up Arms against the British*.[178]

In Chapters One and Three, there is an extensive discussion of terror attacks and political Islam's siege of India. This data adversely portrays the acts in the name of political Islam and the nations at the forefront of jihad sponsorship: Pakistan and Saudi Arabia. This is the kind of data that America needs to mobilize opinion worldwide—data from a non-Christian, non-white developing nation that has been extensively victimized, its civilians killed and its Muslim citizens brainwashed to sponsor terror, all in the name of jihad.

Getting Educated Muslims to Listen

The most effective political Islamists, including jihadis, are invariably educated Muslims. This should surprise no one. It takes modern knowledge to operate effectively in the Western world; a college degree is a good way of obtaining this knowledge. The mainstream media in Muslim majority nations and mosques around the world spew out anti-American and anti-Israeli political literature and often give one-sided, exaggerated or even falsified analysis. This indoctrination, no doubt, has brainwashed most educated Muslims. However, many educated Muslims involved in jihadist attacks abroad also read or listen to mainstream media abroad. Without this reading, they couldn't function effectively in alien societies. However, a lack of critical analysis of Islamic doctrines and Muslim claims of "grievance" in western media has been a setback to the war on terror efforts. This has meant that the one-sided indoctrination carried out on educated Muslims by political Islamists for decades has been left unchallenged.

The first batch of educated Muslims may have been more jihad prone due to this mostly one-sided indoctrination. But the second batch need not be so. Saudis and Muslims from other nations coming for higher studies in western nations would most benefit from the local media and the government propaganda machinery willing to discredit the theological roots of political Islam. These Muslims must be confronted with the reality that information taken down from leaves, stones or people's memory, and written down almost one hundred years later couldn't be accurate or complete enough to be called God's Words. This profound reality, which is not likely to be raised in a Muslim majority nation due to death threats from political Islam, should appeal successfully to the common sense of the educated Muslim elite. Most of these "liberated" Muslims, who form the elite of Islamic nations, will likely work to discredit political Islam upon return to their homelands, setting off a revolution from within. The strategy outlined here is about empowering educated Muslims to successfully confront political Islam.

It is illustrative to study how a critical section of a community or an organization may be influenced in order to initiate a revolution from within. Among the reasons that the white elite in South Africa gave up power to black majority was that whites from Europe and America confronted them (in people-to-people interactions when they encountered each other during travels) and told them that it was immoral for them to keep native blacks illegally away from power. Unable to muster a convincing response, the white South Africans found themselves looked down upon and feared being ostracized by their fellow whites abroad. Increasingly, these South African whites put pressure on their leadership to give up power to blacks.

Aggressive advertisements portraying cigarette smoking as being "cool" when it was understood to be harmful meant that top executives of cigarette companies were being looked down upon by their fellow socialites. This is among the reasons leading to changes in the tone of cigarette advertisements in the United States.

Visitors from the former Soviet Union and its satellites always found themselves in a no-win situation in standing up for their ideology and the economic performance of their nations in front of Western liberty and capitalism. In the long run, the ideology and the system collapsed from within as they ran out of believers.

The executive and legislative branches of the United States should work to rectify the existing situation of meaningless political correctness by calling for a critical look at the theology behind political Islam; its inconsistencies, evident incompleteness, and lack of authenticity should be pointed out (Chapter Two). Political Islamic theology, seen by many Islamists as its greatest strength, is its greatness weakness when seen through the lens of science-derived common sense. This may be the most important long-term strategy in neutralizing political Islam—by discrediting political Islamic theology and by extension clergy and mosques, which make up the nodes of the social network responsible for spawning jihad.

Distance and Discredit Saudi Arabia

Along with Shiite Iran, Saudi Arabia is the dominant ideological and funding source for nodes of social network spawning jihad.

By spending well over $85-90 billion since the mid-1970s through its government and non-governmental organizations, as well as countless more through private Saudis, it is no exaggeration to say that the resurgence of political Islam in the past few decades has been mostly due to Saudi funding and proselytizing activities in favor of Wahhabism.[7] Saudi Arabia is dedicated to empire-building of a different kind. It is using time-tested old-style Islamic conquest to create and expand regions of Saudi influence.

Unlike the former Soviet Union, it has done so in the name of God and has enhanced an inherited ideology called political Islam.

This Saudi empire-building has caused immense suffering to people around the world, including Muslims themselves. Sermons in Saudi-funded mosques have kept millions of Muslims around the world from embracing modern education and being part of larger society or community of nations. It appears that only a tiny fraction of the Saudi money spent on Muslim communities abroad has gone into building mainstream educational institutions and hospitals, which shows where Saudi interests lie.

The long-term policy approach should be one of developing a grievance against Saudi Arabia as the root cause of Muslim sufferings. For instance, propaganda directed at young British Muslims should be toward portraying political Islam, Saudi Arabia, and Pakistan as the root cause of their inability to succeed in British society (Chapter Three).

The western propaganda along these lines should get to those who count in the long run: the educated Muslims. In particular, the nodal power centers of political Islam, the mainstream mosques, need to be identified as doing the bidding for the Saudis, indirectly ensuring the Saudi control of communities. Many nations in Middle East and Africa have lost their religions, languages and culture after Islamic conquest that either originated in or was inspired by Saudi Arabia. The oil wealth has ensured further consolidation of this conquest and the use of these nations and its people for further conquest of "infidel" lands to extend Saudi sphere of influence.

In a nutshell, Saudi Arabia has destroyed the future of hundreds of millions of Muslims around the world. Indeed, Saudi Arabia—not America or Israel—is the real enemy of Muslim nations and Muslim communities.

Being a recipient of free wealth in the form of oil, Saudis could afford to practice a retrogressive form of political Islam as it relies on imported skilled and unskilled labor. The majority of skilled laborers in Saudi Arabia are still foreigners. This is reflection that this nation is offering no future even for its own people, apart from a shrinking share of oil revenue.

America's complex relation with the Saudis dates back to the early 1900s. From an ideological view, this relationship has always been one-sided. The American democracy and church have no access to Saudi Arabia, while Saudis kept a large contingent of religious propagators in its embassy and consulates in America until 2001. The statistics discussed earlier showed significant Saudi contribution to the growth of political Islam in America.[156]

The Saudi Ambassador's regrettable extraordinary access to the sitting and past American presidents is an indication of a nation that does not know the dynamics of political Islam—the de facto power in Saudi Arabia and an arch-enemy of America. It seems that Saudis have known very well which buttons to push in the White House in order to get their jihadi agenda across, even at the expense of America's close allies, such as Israel. In July 2001, a particular Israeli crackdown on Palestinians appeared harsh in Saudi eyes. Through their Ambassador Bandar, the Saudis cautioned President Bush: "The Crown Prince will not communicate in any form, type or shape with you, and Saudi Arabia will take all its political, economic and security decisions based upon how it sees its own interests in the region without taking into account American interests anymore". Swiftly, President Bush wrote back to pledge for the first time: "The Palestinian people have a right to self-determination and to live peacefully and securely in their own state, in their homeland, just as Israelis have the right to live peacefully and safely in their own state".[179]

America continues to benefit tactically through an alliance with a "friendly" monarchy in Saudi Arabia. This includes, for instance, getting Saudi help to limit Iranian influence in the region. But on the larger strategic front America and the monarchy have an opposing world view (America wants to bring development and democracy around the world and Saudi Arabia wants a subservient world through Islamic conquest)—and due to that America is losing on the war on terror. The ruling elite in Saudi Arabia that consists of the monarchy and the Wahhabi clergy can keep their powerbase, prestige and wealth only by maintaining political Islam's influence within the nation. But political Islam is an inherently destabilizing force, repressing the Saudi population and sponsoring jihad worldwide through an immense oil-derived wealth. With time and resources no longer on its side, America is now forced to look at the larger strategic goals vis-à-vis Saudi Arabia.

As part of a winning war strategy, the enemy must be put on the defensive; we must turn the tables on nations such as Saudi Arabia and Pakistan by pointing out their policies of exporting extreme versions of Islam, their own bloody record of jihad directed at non-Muslims, and that they are yet to be held accountable.

Like it did with Soviet Union, America has no choice but to launch a propaganda drive aimed at discrediting and isolating Saudi Arabia. With over 15 percent of American oil imports coming from this adversary, this is not an easy decision. But the time may have come to try some innovative ideas designed to overcome the well-exploited oil weakness.

America can no longer afford to avoid recognizing Saudi Arabia as the primary nation behind jihad. The indecisive measures that have been taken until now will only make the terror war more difficult to manage in near future as the Sunni-Shia conflict intensifies. The cost of fighting this war (already about a trillion dollars) and what is yet to come if Saudi Arabia is not effectively confronted may surpass the cost of temporary or short-term disturbance to oil flow from the Middle East. In subsequent sections, we will consider some non-military and military options regarding Saudi Arabia.

Dealing with Iran

America may have to launch military strikes in order to take out the Iranian nuclear infrastructure, or at least slow down its nuclear program. In a *Washington Post* op-ed, Vali Nasr and Ray Takeyh articulate: "United States would do better to shelve its containment strategy and embark on a policy of unconditional dialogue and sanctions relief."[180] In this book's view, such a policy would only embolden and empower political Islam—that is, both the power base and part of the ruling clique through the clergy. These authors' suggestions could lead to an Iran that is far more powerful and still adversarial to the western interests.

The ex-CIA Director James Woolsey rejects the Baker-Hamilton Iraq Study Group's proposal, which advocates engaging Iran and Syria "constructively." He says this would "legitimize their regimes, embolden them and their terrorist cohorts, buy time for Iran's nuclear weapons program, and create the illusion of useful effort and thus discourage more effective steps." He also suggests that America hit the Iranian leadership with travel and financial sanctions, and seek to bring charges against President Mahmoud Ahmadinejad in an international tribunal for "violation of the Genocide Convention in calling publicly for the destruction of Israel."[181]

Kenneth Timmerman advocates: "We should enforce the huge number of judgments against top regime leaders in courts around the world for their terrorist attacks."[181]

In the long run, a different policy direction vis-à-vis Iran may be advisable. Roya Hakakian, writing in the *Wall Street Journal,* points out interesting statistics released by Tehran's office of cultural affairs "showing a dramatic drop in the number of Iranians who pray daily". There is also the growing popularity of pre-Islamic festivals such as *Nowrooz—* a traditional Iranian New Year Celebration.[182]

Mainstream education in Shiite Iran was made far more modern and inclusive than the one in Sunni majority Saudi Arabia, due to the realization even among Ayatollahs that a strong Iran requires a more modern education. This has made a segment of the Iranian population, especially the educated class, open to infusions of new knowledge. This decision by the mullahs has an inadvertent consequence: the educated in Iran, disenchanted with the overly religious ruling elite, develop a yearning for a secular and modern leadership.[183]

This Iranian population may be ready to embrace the view of clergy as enforcers of Arab imperialism called political Islam on Iranian people, keeping Iran and its people from developing and reaching their potential (see the Section titled *Discredit and Distance Saudi Arabia*).

In the event of an America-led military strike on Iran that would neutralize its nuclear capability, the responsibility for the resulting damage must be pinned on the ruling mullahs and political Islamic ideology. It can be stated that had Iran practiced *Bhai* (pre-Islamic) faith, it might not have become a pariah and a dysfunctional nation. In particular, an anti-Arab campaign may single out those with black turban, signifying claims of lineage to Islam's Arab founder, Mohammed. This may even include Hassan Nasrallah, the chief of Hizbollah, an Iranian proxy.

In the meantime, the U.S. should continue the policy of aiding states or groups targeted by Iran-sponsored proxies: be it Fatah, targeted by Hamas or the beleaguered Lebanese government, under pressure from Hizbollah. The U.S. should also continue targeting Iranian agents inside Iraq.

Decreasing oil revenues, in addition to economic sanctions, could put pressure on the ruling clergy in Iran to make concessions. However, it is only by weakening political Islam within Iran that the U.S. and allies can hope to neutralize the Iranian nuclear or terror threat.

Neutralize Power Base of Political Islam

As a primary target of political Islam, America needs to take the lead in moving beyond an ineffective focus on radical Islam and going after power structures that sustain and promote political Islam. As has been emphasized here, political Islam must first be neutralized simply to win the war on terror, let alone for democracy to take root or for a civilized order to be established.

The jihadis, otherwise known as violent activists of political Islam, are radicalized by Muslim clerics (Islamic scholars are also considered clerics due to their knowledge of the Islamic trilogy) in mainstream mosques. Hence, it is appropriate to consider Muslim clerics as the leaders of political Islam. The institutions clerics head, be they mosques, seminaries, or *madarasas*, are power structures or nodes of political Islam. Clerical association with and propagation of scriptures in the trilogy (Chapter Two) that instigate unprovoked violence against the non-Muslim citizens of the United States imply a requirement to purposefully and materially support hostilities against the United States. Also, there could be grounds for viewing these portions of the Islamic trilogy and their consequential track record around the world as constituting politically-motivated hate crime.[184]

One could argue that scriptures belonging to other faiths also urge violent attacks against people of alternate faiths at times. How could America or any other non-Muslim nation be justified and not be seen as biased in going only after political Islam-influenced religious institutions, as opposed to, say, Hindu or Buddhist religious institutions? Singling out the Taliban or Al-Qaeda as enemy entities in the

Military Commissions Act (see below) is a reflection of the identification of the problem in Islam, which, again, has no parallel in other religions. In an earlier Section titled *Right to Exist*, arguments distinguishing political Islam from other faiths are given, along with the right of preemption as means of neutralizing political Islam.

America can give yet another reason for shutting down political Islam-influenced institutions: the lack of reciprocity in prominent Islamic nations that are under strong political Islamic influence—specifically Saudi Arabia, Iran, and Pakistan—is a reflection of the expansionist and exclusivist nature of political Islam and its religious institutions.

Either cutting off or slowing down Saudi funding or funding from other Islamic nations is having little effect, as political Islam is able to sustain itself through local Muslim support. Hence, it is suggested here that America use one of its new laws to shut down the operation of nodal power structures of political Islam operating within its jurisdiction.

Power structures of political Islam, or political Islam-influenced religious institutions, is taken here to mean any Muslim religious institution that stocks, distributes or propagates the Islamic trilogy of the Koran, Hadith and Sira or any material derived from it.

A detailed analysis of these issues within the context of local and international law is outside the scope of this book. We will discuss only the parameters under which existing or new laws could be enacted to shut down political Islam-inspired religious institutions.

The Military Commissions Act of 2006 may allow the executive branch to wage an effective war on political Islam by categorizing Muslim clerics as unlawful enemy combatants and shutting down their place of operations, which could be any Islamic religious institution, association, or organization. Either in this form or in a modified one, this Act could be a basis for other nations to wage an effective war on political Islam. This Act allows for "alien unlawful enemy combatants ... [to be] subject to trial by military commissions" without the constitutional safeguards that American citizens possess against illegal detainment and due process. Moreover, the Act allows "pain or suffering incidental to lawful sanctions" and "statements ... obtained by coercion".[185]

The term "unlawful enemy combatant" means: (i) a person who has engaged in hostilities or who has purposefully and materially supported hostilities against the United States or its co-belligerents and is not a lawful enemy combatant (including a person who is part of the Taliban, Al-Qaeda, or associated forces); or (ii) a person who, before, on, or after the date of the enactment of the Military Commissions Act of 2006, has been determined to be an unlawful enemy combatant by a Combatant Status Review Tribunal or another competent tribunal established under the authority of the president or the secretary of defense. [185]

Jose Padilla—a U.S. citizen born and bred in America—was arrested in 2002, and a District Court upheld the President's authority to designate any person, citizen or alien, an "enemy combatant" and to detain such a person indefinitely.[185]

Shutting down Muslim religious organizations that have clerics in administrative roles greatly reduces effective ways of preaching political Islamic ideas and aids in preempting jihad buildup.

There is also no reason why the U.S. Congress couldn't enact legislation or use existing laws to shut down political Islam-influenced virtual mosques on the Internet.[186] Simply put, there is no justifiable reason for an alien ideology such as political Islam to take root and expand in non-Muslim nations, given this ideology's contemporary and widespread track record of unbeliever genocide and its repression of Muslims. Under this scenario, once the nodes of political Islam are neutralized, the American Muslim population should be exposed to an objective—and justifiably negative—view of political Islam, both at the community level and in the media, and an expose' of Saudi Arabia. This could lead to political Islam's unraveling and a Muslim exodus to alternate ways of life. Such an American policy initiative should embolden the rest of the unbeliever world.

Of course, if America starts shutting down political Islam-influenced mosques, there will be a hue and cry in the Muslim world. This is a given. Most Muslim governments will be under pressure to stop "cooperating" with America. It is important to realize that most governments in the Muslim world either represent political Islam or are prisoners of it. Clearly, we have to do our homework right by first building up a campaign to take down political Islam and undercut the axis of jihad nations. This should reduce the short-term price America has to pay to win the war on terror.

Aid Allies

The strategy outlined above, all by itself, may not be effective in non-Muslim nations where the Muslim population is a sizeable percentage of the total population and has a high growth rate and where political Islam is entrenched among Muslims. The nations facing this demographic threat from political Islam may not have time on their side.

As was discussed in the previous Chapter, Europe is under a serious threat from political Islam. Some of the steps enacted by European nations in response to Islamic radicalism, such as the requirement to preach in national language in local mosques, is too little and too late. These steps do little to significantly weaken political Islam and to help assimilate Muslims into the mainstream.

Of all the European nations, France faces the gravest challenge by far, with one in three or four babies now being born to Muslim immigrants—an indication of the magnitude and the time-bound nature of the demographic threat (previous Chapter). When a civilization faces annihilation from an enemy political ideology masquerading as a religion, innovative solutions must be found.

Under these circumstances, an overarching human rights principle could be invoked—that is, the right of civilizations to exist as entities in their homelands. This means sending the threatening alien civilization in ethnic ghettos back to their native lands voluntarily or by creating conditions through the use of force. Unfortunately, this is bound to create hardship for the displaced population and its descendents. But this population and the nation(s) they came from are not entirely blameless, having deliberately refused to assimilate and becoming a genocidal threat to the generous host nation.

Israel too faces a similar challenge, with the native Arab Muslim population fast outpacing Jews in growth rates.

Being a small nation both in population and in area, Israel faces another threat from adjacent Muslim majority Palestinian territories of West Bank and Gaza.

The lack of recognition of Israel and threats to annihilate it comes not just from Arab Muslim nations, but also from Iran and in mosques in far away Indonesia—nations that do not even share boundaries with the Jewish state. Indeed, the inability to accept Israel or the existence of Jews in Middle East is deeply rooted in the trilogy, going all the way back to Islam's founder, Mohammed.

The fact that political Islam is really, first and foremost, a front for Arab expansion and conquest (even at the expense of non-Arab Muslims), and how unfairly Israel is singled out is exemplified in several ways. Here is one. In the Darfur region of Sudan, Arab tribes are in the process of conquesting land belonging to black African Muslims and others. At a March 2007 meeting of the newly formed UN Human Rights Council, acording to a report in the *New York Times*:

> Organization of the Islamic Conference, an association of 57 states promoting Muslim solidarity, have dashed those hopes by voting as a bloc to stymy Western efforts to direct serious attention to situations like the killings, rapes and pillage in the Darfur region of Sudan, which the United Nations has declared the world's worst humanitarian crisis. Most notably, as happened with the commission, the council has focused its condemnation almost exclusively on Israel. It has passed eight resolutions against Israel, and the Islamic group is planning four more for the current

session. The council has cited no other country for human rights violations.[187]

Daniel Pipes makes an eloquent point regarding Israel's enemies: "One does not, in fact, make peace with one's enemy; one makes peace with one's former enemy." [188] In this book's view, the enemy in this case is political Islamic movement, with Fatah or Hamas, among its many manifestations. As long as political Islam is the power broker in Middle East, any attempts to settle the Israel-Palestinian conflict appear to be unwise.

Blaming Israelis for self-induced deficiencies while calling itself a victim is part of the Palestinian strategy of waging jihad. Arguably, the Arab-Israeli conflict can be seen as a religious war on an "infidel" nation and an attempt at conquest of the Jewish land. For humanitarian considerations and for strategic reasons, American policy must be geared toward a long-lasting Jewish state in the Middle East, with the acknowledgement that Arabs in Israel, the West Bank, and Gaza could be absorbed in nearby Arab states. This formula once again ensures the right of civilizations to exist and punishes those who conduct jihad.

As part of an ideological offense, America could encourage internal movements in nations such as France or Israel toward these types of human rights-based innovative solutions.

Turkey, which has a vast Muslim majority, has strong secular traditions—a remnant of Kemal Ataturk's legacy. This tradition is under a serious threat. The ruling Islamic party has been systematically promoting Islamism through various means. For instance, this party's support for the establishment of religious schools meant that political Islam will be increasingly taught to Turkey's children. This will result in gradual Islamization of Turkey. Looking at it from a different perspective, political Islam is using the ballot box to reach power and is gradually consolidating its position by promoting all-too-familiar religious "values".

A concerned military leadership and segments of the public in Turkey are making a last-ditch effort to save themselves and their nation from political Islam. In April 2007, Ankara and Istanbul saw huge demonstrations by secularists against the ruling Islamic party and government. Both Europe and Washington should do better than to follow a hands-off policy, letting the "democracy take its course". Instead, the developing situation in Turkey should be seen as political Islamic siege on Turkey and its democracy, undoubtedly aided by long-term Saudi funding for political Islamic causes there. This situation should be seen as an opportunity both to assist the secularists in Turkey and to drive a wedge between political Islam and the Turks. A propaganda drive may be formulated along the lines that the encroaching of political Islam in Turkey can be seen as a Saudi effort to bring Turkey under its wing, impose an Arabian tribal way of life, and compromise the future of millions of Turks.

Jihad as a Crime Against Humanity

Nations represent people and their interests. It is therefore not surprising for them to behave like humans. The hallmark of a secure and functional society is a robust criminal justice system; the hallmark of a functional international order is an international justice system that works. These are among the reasons that the Geneva Convention was established.

When violent jihad involves terrorism—which it almost always does—these acts fall under the category of war crimes. As we saw in Chapter One, many non-state terror sponsors, such as Al-Qaeda, thrive either through state sponsorship or because states turn a blind eye when their residents sponsor terror. When these crimes are planned or committed in a systematic fashion and on a large scale, they may be prosecuted under crimes against humanity as defined by the Geneva Convention.

A complete listing of all breaches is beyond the scope of this book. Only a few of them are listed to inform the reader that acts of jihad can be persecuted under the Convention. Article 3 and 4 of the Geneva Convention deals with acts constituting war crimes.[189] There is also an internal component, applicable to crimes conducted by home-grown jihadis.

Grave Breaches—International (of the four Geneva Conventions of August 12, 1949):

o Willful killing
o Extensive destruction and appropriation of property, not justified by military necessity and carried out unlawfully and wantonly
o Taking of hostages

Other Serious Violations (of laws and customs applicable in international armed conflict):

- o Intentionally directing attacks against the civilian population as such or against individual civilians not taking direct part in hostilities
- o Intentionally directing attacks against civilian objects, that is, objects which are not military objectives

In the last sixty years, non-Muslims have been systematically and violently driven out of many Muslim majority areas. This has happened due to state sponsorship. However, there is hardly any discussion in media about these crimes or their implications.

To take one example, Pakistan has a long history of conducting jihad against "infidels" (Sections: *Axis of Jihad* and *Siege of India*). An apparent admission of Pakistan's sponsorship of jihad in Kashmir came in a 2006 lecture at the South Asia Program of the School of Advanced International Studies of Johns Hopkins University by Pakistan's Ambassador to the United States, Mahmud Ali Durrani: "Jihad, insurgency or whatever you want to call it in Kashmir... Yes, Pakistan may have helped the jihad at some time, but it was not started by us".[190]

Milosevic and his cronies were tried on crimes against humanity charges, ironically, conducted mostly against Kosovar Muslims. But many deserving Muslim Milosevics are yet to be even identified. Clearly, not only individuals, but many Islamic states have been involved in jihad. Some progress has been made in passing judgments against the state sponsorship of genocide. In a 15-1 landmark judgment that the 16-member International Court of Justice delivered on February 26, 2007, it was ruled for the first time that states can be held responsible for genocide (till now, only individuals have been held responsible). But this judgment may have exposed the limitation of the international justice system, which went by the letter rather than the spirit of the international conventions. This means that as long as states did not keep a documented trail of their intent, they may be able to escape conviction.[191]

An analysis and publicizing of jihad as a crime against humanity, as we will see, should strengthen the legal and moral standing of America and its allies in their long battle with political Islam. It also creates a new and powerful way of putting pressure on state sponsors of jihad. Importantly, this could become an effective mobilizing tool, by creating a sense of grievance in the minds of jihad victims against jihad-sponsoring nations and their local collaborators.

We have seen in first chapter how the nations comprising the axis of jihad have made a mockery of the international justice system and have repeatedly and without remorse waged violent jihad on unbelievers. These nations, dominated by political Islam, justify these atrocities in the name of God and as part of the "freedom struggle". In January 2006, India, a long-standing victim of Saudi-sponsored terror, approached the Arab nation to sign an extradition treaty covering terrorism. The Indians needed this because many Saudis, including expatriate Indian Muslims and Pakistanis based in Saudi Arabia, have been involved in India-directed terrorism. But Saudis demanded that India agree to incorporate "freedom struggles" as a justification of acts of violence.[192] This exclusion meant anyone attacking India and killing Indians in the name of Indian Muslims is exempt from the extradition! In other words, Muslim "freedom struggle" is an integral part of Saudi-sponsored jihad.

Of course, it is the Saudis who spent billions on Muslim residents in non-Muslim nations (including India), teaching them to hate the majority and to prevent them joining the mainstream. Saudi funding, along with Pakistani logistics, helped to instill hatred of "infidel" India in the minds of Kashmiri Muslims, and eventually led to over 300,000 non-Muslims being driven out of the region.[93] Many of the killed non-Muslim Kashmiris were first identified for liquidation in local mosques. With Saudi Arabia funding most of these mosques, these killings or attacks may implicate the kingdom in potential crimes against humanity charges.[193] Also, according to Subash Kapila, Saudi Arabia is also indirectly sponsoring jihad against India by "subsidizing Pakistan's (India-specific) terrorism training infrastructure and ISI terrorist operations by a whole host of Islamic fundamentalist terrorist outfits".[194]

One can note how thoughtfully Saudis are framing and carrying out jihad abroad. In reality, the "freedom struggle" in South Asia by Muslims, which Saudi Arabia has sponsored, has become front for marginalizing non-Muslims. Hence, this raises credibility questions when Saudi Arabia claims to support the "freedom struggle" in other parts of the world, including its support for Palestinians in the Israel-Palestinian conflict. This gives credence to the alternate view: Saudis are using the freedom struggle bogey as a cover to drive Jews out from their ancient land—the unfinished chapter of the trilogy—through a jihad conducted by their Palestinian proxies. This shows the extent of the commitment that Saudi

Arabia has towards crimes conducted against humanity, which is in violation of international and local laws.

The continued sponsorship of terror by America's purported "allies," Saudi Arabia and Pakistan, gives an inevitable impression of America being considered a "useful idiot" by these two nations. Saudis have played the victim card skillfully on behalf of the Palestinians. Playing the victim while victimizing unbeliever nations in ways that have included the genocide of non-Muslims at an unprecedented scale in modern times (Chapter One, Section: *Axis of Jihad*), Pakistan has manipulated America to the tune of billions of dollars in aid and in deadly armaments, without any benchmark results to show for it. According to Selig Harrison, since 2001 Pakistan has milked America to the tune of $27.5 billion dollars.[195] After Iraq, Pakistan has received the most aid from America. Agreeing to massively aid and arm a still jihad-sponsoring Pakistan with advanced offensive American weaponry must be reassuring to the Pakistani religious and military elite that terrorism pays![196]

Terrorism expert Gunaratna and others have called for more western investments in Pakistan in order to ensure that its economy continues to grow at the current high growth rate.[197] This suggestion, if implemented, will surely further empower Pakistan and make it far more formidable.

But the proponents of this idea have not given a clear answer how this externally sponsored Pakistan's buildup will make it less of a terror base in the long run. Specifically, there is virtually no discussion on how political Islam (not just radical Islam) within Pakistan will be weakened or neutralized.[197] Some of the most educated and wealthy people in Pakistan are backers of jihad—from its nuclear scientists, businessmen to the top officials of its intelligence (ISI). As it has been pointed out in this book political Islam is the overriding and entrenched power in Pakistan.

We know from our collective experience of a thousand year human history that rewarding criminal behavior as the dominant response almost never reforms a criminal. This book cautions against either arming or building up Pakistan in any way or form at this time and suggests policies that specifically weaken political Islam within Pakistan as part of an integral approach to the war on terror.

The new democrat-controlled Congress is taking a much-needed second look at America's relations with Pakistan and Saudi Arabia. In the proposed legislation now before the Congress, three countries have been singled out on the need to show accountability with regard to terror sponsorship: Pakistan, Afghanistan and Saudi Arabia. The new provisions form part of the Implementation of 9/11 Commission Recommendations Act of 2007, which is aimed at revamping the U.S. national security and foreign policy apparatus to address challenges post-9/11.[198]

The earlier indictment of Saudi Arabia came in the form of the Saudi Arabia Accountability Act of 2005, which was introduced by Senator Arlen Specter. This Act was intended to "halt Saudi support for institutions that fund, train, incite, encourage, or in any other way aid and abet terrorism, and to secure full Saudi cooperation in the investigation of terrorist incidents, and for other purposes."[199] This Act never saw the light of day.

Emboldened by the lack of accountability Saudi and Pakistani jihad sponsorship continued for decades and finally led to 9/11 attacks on America. Yet American policy response to the dastardly 9/11 attack has been one of accommodating and appeasing nations such as Saudi Arabia and Pakistan. Needless to say, such an approach is fundamentally flawed, although one may argue that the want of policy options led to making the deal with the "devils".

As part of a new set of directions suggested here, the policy focus should now be geared toward making the axis of jihad nations accountable for their crimes against humanity.

Jihadis may not fear death, but their backers sitting in air-conditioned villas in Saudi Arabia, Pakistan, and Iran do, and they have much to lose. In other words, the threat of retaliation or preemption can work, as long as it is delivered at the right place and at the right time.

In future, if an attack in a non-Muslim nation is attributed to jihadis and if Saudi Arabia had been involved in indoctrination of the local Muslim community from where jihadis originated, the victim nation could send a bill for damages suffered to Saudi Arabia and follow it up with a military response if need be. The victim nation could also demand that Saudi Arabia, through its religious leadership, issue a statement telling Muslims in the victim nation to desist from taking the relevant verses in the Koran seriously and to stop jihad. The point is, there is a role in which Saudi Arabia could take corrective measures for its past misdeeds, and there is room for taking responsibility. These options need to be further explored in order to build up our leverage on the Saudis.

As part of this approach, America needs to help victim nations of the axis of jihad develop and build local lawsuits seeking damages for the acts of terror. The victim nations include America, Israel, India, the Philippines, Lebanon,

Thailand, England, France, Russia and others. Indeed, multiple lawsuits directed at Saudi Arabia from many nations, including developing ones, spells nothing but consolidation of victims against jihad, which is the first step toward a more unified response.

Successful lawsuits and evidence could potentially be used as a basis to take the following extreme steps as a last resort: seize oil assets in the case of Saudi Arabia or Iran, and land in the case of Pakistan.

India as a Counterforce to Axis of Jihad

While obeying no rules, state sponsors of political Islamic terror, through their proxies, have successfully managed to impose an asymmetric war on America and its Western allies, including Israel. Also, by exploiting Israel's occasional and difficult-to-avoid excesses on Palestinians, jihadist nations have created a guilt complex to restrain America's policy towards terror. Time and again, Europeans who are mired in socialism, with few or no expendable youngsters, have not shown the stomach for a fight. Diverging interests have made the UN Security Council ineffective. Under the current circumstances, America alone is no longer capable of containing the entrenched and expansionist political Islamic forces in Saudi Arabia, Iran or Pakistan.

As a nation of law, America's ability to respond to this "dirty war" will likely remain constrained (and therefore indecisive) as long as jihadis restrict themselves to a war of thousand cuts, as opposed to nuclear strikes directed at

American interests. But not all victim states of Islamic terror are obligated to respond with restraint.

Data and analysis presented in *Axis of Jihad* and *Siege of India* sections make it unequivocally clear that non-Muslim Indians, specifically majority "infidel" Hindus, are in a death-fight with Islamic forces as commanded by Pakistan and Saudi Arabia. Understandably, non-Muslims are terrified of political Islam in South Asia. As a matter of survival in a nation where the rule of law is not supreme, India's population has shown willingness to engage in a "dirty war" with Islamists. In other words, political Islamic thuggery can find its match in the form of India, if Washington can help to script this. In a nutshell, this is about leveraging the collective will of 850 million cornered Indians to take the war to the jihadists and their sponsoring states.

If America could help deliver a fatal blow to the former Soviet Union by backing Muslim nations against the Soviet occupation of Afghanistan, why not back cornered Indians to fight political Islam and its sponsoring nations? Unlike a resurgent political Islam, which has turned its guns on its former benefactor America, a resurgent India already sharing secular and democratic mode of governing is no threat to the Western civilization.

In terms of population, location and size, India matches the extended global network of Muslim populations that are influenced by political Islam. As discussed before, when a non-white, non-Christian developing nation such as India claims to have been victimized at the hands of Islamic nations, it is bound to create ideological difficulties for Islamists who have made Muslim grievance the bedrock upon which to build the jihad castle. Inserting India and Indians into a prominent role in the war on terror and propagating Indian sufferings in the hands of political Islam should have another benefit: the left in both Europe and America will take a second look at their sympathy for Islamists.

The strategic importance of successfully repulsing political Islam in India is immeasurable. It will put a full stop to the geo-political goal of bringing radicals together, from Indonesia to Algeria, on a contiguous landmass. As conquest is the primary passion of axis of jihad and their sidekicks, this will be an immense blow. An India working to successfully neutralize political Islam within can do more. Sharing language and culture with Pakistan and Bangladesh, such an India could help to liberate these nations to alternate faiths and ways of life. The hugely popular Hindi movies made in India can be used de-program Muslims in India, Pakistan, Afghanistan and Bangladesh away from political Islam and can help to mobilize unbelievers against the Islamist threat. While these ideas may look far-fetched now, policy decisions should be geared toward rapidly building up India in order to create a new future.

India has significant land claims over Pakistan, land that is owed because of non-Muslim expulsions to India.[121] India also must have substantial compensation claims over Saudi Arabia for its sponsorship of extensive jihad in India. Hence, India may be justified in hitting back and helping to achieve a decisive shift in the war on terror.

This book suggests a rapid build-up of India as a counter-force to political Islam and its sponsors. In the event of an oil embargo against India, as part of an integral strategy, America must be able to step in to fulfill India's limited needs. A side point to be noted is that an India that is increasingly destabilized by Islamic forces will be unlikely to counter-balance China in the region.

There is much work to be done, with India currently suffering under a dysfunctional democracy that is being overrun by Islamists (Chapter Three). But that can be changed by American backing of Indian nationalists and by realizing that Indian democracy will not overcome this losing trend on its own. By indoctrinating Indian Muslims, Pakistan and Saudi Arabia have turned them against the Indian state. The Indian state and non-Muslim Indians are made to feel that they are occupiers in Muslim-majority regions and towns of India. Stefan Halper writes in the *Washington Times*: "Since World War II, with hardly any exceptions, insurgencies have succeeded against occupying democratic powers."[200]

The conventional wisdom is India is rising (thanks to building quality technical and professional higher educational institutions in 1950s and 60s, recent wealth creation has become feasible) despite the otherwise poorly governing state.[201] Not surprisingly, in areas where governance is required—such as providing security—Indian democracy has failed to perform. This should not be a surprise any more (see the section titled *Democracy Through Wealth Creation*, Chapter One). Democracy as a mode of governing in developing nations has been a failure, almost without exception.

Culturally, religiously, and in terms of nation-building, Indians are much closer to East Asians than Middle Easterners or Africans. Like East Asians, Indian immigrants in Western countries have done very well, unlike the immigrants of Middle Eastern or African origin or even immigrants from Muslim majority regions of Pakistan or

Bangladesh. Hence, we shouldn't fear that an undemocratic but a visionary government in New Delhi—which is a must under the circumstances—would misrule India.

As discussed in the previous chapter, political Islam is making rapid strides in India because the Hindu majority is disunited and politically divided. An India destabilized by Pakistan and Saudi Arabia (as well as China, possibly, and now Iran too may be entering the fray) needs counter-balancing forces in the form of the Western nations. Helping India is nothing other than helping to empower a West-friendly Hindu majority to mobilize and take on political Islam. This also involves aiding Hindu organizations and promoting able and strong leaders such as Narendra Modi of Bharathya Janata Party (BJP), which have the wherewithal to take on political Islam. Polls have shown Modi as the most admired chief minister in India.[202]

Backing the Congress party in India is to back a political-Islam promoting party (either inadvertently or otherwise), which, unlike BJP, according to Indian intelligence, has been infiltrated by jihadis.[122]

The author's *Washington Times* letter articulates the need for a new U.S. policy response vis-à-vis India:

Jihadist threat in India

The timely editorial welcoming the formal signing of U.S.-Indian nuclear ties is notable for its foresightedness ("U.S.-India nuclear ties," yesterday). However, jihadis and their sponsors have voiced displeasure over the emerging close ties between the two nations. This deserves close attention.

Pakistan and the usual suspects from Middle East have made a passionate 30-plus-year effort to indoctrinate, establish and fund terror cells in Indian Muslim communities. This investment toward Islamic conquest of "infidels" is finally paying off. In the beginning of 2007, according to the Indian home minister nations nuclear installations are on an Islamic terror hit list along with oil refineries. Prime Minister Manmohan Singh's regime, elected through a voting bloc controlled by jihadis, has been more than accommodating toward them. This regime even has rescinded an anti-terror law and has made India's ability to defeat radical Islam difficult. A disorganized and divided Hindu majority has been taken advantage of by united jihadis.

In the long run, if the United States wants an effective ally in India and wants democracy to succeed there, it must side with Hindu-majority organizations and help them undermine Indian jihadis. Otherwise, the trend in intensifying Islamic terrorism and its siege of Indian democracy shows that the promise of U.S.-Indian ties likely will go unfulfilled and jihadis will destroy another critical democratic ally in South Asia.[203]

In this book's view, the Bush administration's focus on clinching a nuclear deal with India is unwarranted, given the large time scales—10-15 years to build nuclear reactors—involved. The matter of priority is building up India rapidly to take on the jihadi threat; without that, it is this author's view that India will be stabilized by Islamic forces irrecoverably and we will lose the opportunity to leverage 850 million Indians for a win-win situation in the war on terror and beyond.

Scope for Nuclear Retaliation

A nuclear device smuggled through American ports could be among the likely ways a nuclear attack might be carried out on American soil. The Department of Homeland Security has been aware of this possibility and is looking into setting up a massive system of radiation detectors in many American ports.[204] However, the yearly trillion dollars of complex trade and nuclear proliferation initiated by Pakistan is likely to keep American ports vulnerable for years to come.

The physics and technology of making a nuclear bomb is old and known to many countries. A nation determined to build an infrastructure that is geared toward achieving nuclear threshold may just get there—ask Pakistan, North Korea or possibly even Iran, a few years down the road. The United States and its allies may be successful in slowing the Iranian momentum toward the bomb, but are unlikely to stop it completely without a full-scale invasion. Thanks to its likely funding of the Pakistani nuke program, Saudi Arabia may already have nukes.[10] This has created tricky policy options in Washington and in European capitals. It is not just the Islamists; even secular nationalist Iranians want the bomb. But the trigger in the hands of a volatile, Islamist and rhetorical Ahmadinejad has caused great deal of concern.

Israel should feel particularly threatened, with Ahmadinejad virulently questioning the need for its existence. Many Sunni Arab states are also getting restless about the Iranian nuclear thrust and have started clamoring for nuclear energy, which is a step toward achieving nuclear bomb making capability.[205]

The fact that the primary jihad-sponsoring nations either have nukes or are close to achieving the threshold is truly a nightmare come true. Pakistan's acquiring of nuclear weapons and spreading the nuclear technology was for an "ideological" cause, taken to mean jihad; this was admitted by none other than the disgraced Pakistani nuclear scientist Qadeer Khan himself.[206] No doubt, some jihadis see distribution of nukes among Muslim nations as desirable both for waging jihad and finally for attacking America with nukes at an opportune time.

Even Arab nations may not see a nuclear-armed Israel as a threat to their existence. The reason is simple: Israel does not believe in an ideology similar to political Islam like its Arab neighbors do. Thus, the long-term solution to Muslim nuclear threat is to discredit the ideological basis of political Islam itself (Chapter Two).

It is not clear what the American response would be if a nuke goes off in the mainland, Europe or in Israel. Analyzing nuclear material left over after the blast to look for "signatures" and determining the origin of the material has become increasingly feasible.[207] But on the downside, this approach is not only time-consuming, but is unreliable in a world in which nuclear technology has proliferated.

The following can be part of an immediate response in the event of a nuclear strike on American mainland. The United States responds with massive strategic strikes on most Saudi Arabian, Iranian and Pakistani cities. Although these nations may not have been directly involved in a strike on America, they have for years contributed to the growth of hatred of America, have sponsored the likes of Taliban, Hizbollah or Al-Qaeda, and/or have proliferated nuclear technology among Islamic nations. Such a response would mean America's policy of "engaging" Pakistan or Saudi Arabia had ultimately failed, and that the time had come to decisively take care of this threat. Not having paid any significant price, none of these societies have seriously scaled back jihad; it has only been diverted. These strikes should make these states accountable for decades of sponsoring jihad and crimes against humanity—and has the potential to set forth a new beginning in these nations and Islam around the world.

Other than the short-term devastating consequences of blast heat associated with a nuclear strike, the long-term medical impact may be limited. Studies of surviving populations in Hiroshima and Nagasaki, exposed to nuclear strikes during Second World War, have shown them to be without significant long-term or genetic effects.[208] Hence, for all practical purposes, a nuclear strike is equivalent to the synergy of thousands of conventional bombs exploding at the same time and at the same point.

It is worth considering whether American leadership should privately notify these nations of the existence of such a policy. Nuclear annihilation is one thing even the jihadist elite can't afford, as it negates their primary goal: worldwide domination of Islam through jihad. If Saudi Arabia or Iran could spend hundreds of billions to spread messages of hatred against the West, they may be persuaded to spend some to create goodwill towards the West and to restrain nations such as Pakistan ideologically if they face an impending threat of nuclear annihilation. Also, with this notification, these nations may be reluctant to further proliferate nuclear technology or carry on with jihad as usual.

Jihadis are also developing arguments to justify nuking America. A refined effort from a legal standpoint has been advanced by a Saudi jihadist Nasir Bin Hamad al-Fahd in a 2003 document called *A Treatise on the Law on the use of Weapons of Mass Destruction Against Unbelievers*. This jihadist asserts that under the conditions of Muslim military inferiority, warfare methods violating laws of jihad can be used. "If the unbelievers can be repelled" only by using Weapons of Mass Destruction (WMD), then "their use is permissible, even if you kill them without exception". He softened his proposals by saying that Muslims fighting jihad may not inflict disproportionately more harm on the enemy than the enemy inflicted on them. "Some brothers have added up the number of Muslims killed directly or indirectly by [American] weapons and come up with a figure of nearly 10 million". This total would authorize the use of WMD to kill about 10 million Americans.[209]

Some jihadis may prefer extensive bleeding of certain "infidel" nations through terror or through other forms of jihad, rather than resorting to nuclear strikes. Under what conditions can America, Israel or India, the primary targets of political Islam, strike back preemptively with strategic nuclear weapons? Before even thinking about a devising a policy along these lines, we must be prepared. Enemy nations, such as axis of jihad, needs to be identified; laundry list of grievances needs to be publicized; and the theological roots of political Islam need to be discredited. It is estimated that Saudi Arabia owes America upwards of a trillion dollars in damages for either directly or indirectly sponsoring terrorism against its interests and its citizens.[210] The victim list can be further expanded to include Israel, India, Russia and many others, who may be owed from several tens of billions to several hundreds of billions of dollars in damages.

In determining preemptive measures, what needs to be factored also is the extent of damage yet to occur through jihad in the years and decades ahead. With largest petroleum reserves anywhere in the world expected to last several decades and with no viable fuel alternative yet to be found, Saudis will have the wealth to sponsor jihad. There should be plenty of jihadis emanating from Saudi Arabia, due to a high population growth rate derived from over four children born on the average to every Saudi woman.[211] The extent of clerical grip on its society will likely ensure that Saudis do not get well-rounded and modern education, maintaining jihad and its sponsorship among the desired professions. A classified American intelligence report, taken from a Saudi intelligence survey in mid-October 2002 of educated Saudis between the ages of 25 and 41, concluded that 95 percent of them supported Bin Laden's cause.[212] Pakistan, with a similarly high population growth rate and a long track record of genocide against unbelievers, will be more than happy to be Saudi Arabia's favorite outsourced nation for jihad. These polls and Pakistan's track record reflect the undeniable: violent jihad is deeply and overwhelmingly enshrined in these societies.

These statistics point to nations inhabited by populations capable of conducting and sponsoring genocide of unbelievers through jihad. With this national dynamics, having America "friendly" rulers is largely irrelevant and it's borne by the reality: continued sponsorship of jihad from these nations.

Why jihad is a thriving enterprise among Muslim communities even in Britain, let alone in Saudi Arabia or Pakistan, is exemplified in this interview with a former British jihadi, Hassan Butt: "He became one of the network's star fundraisers... Butt says he openly told them he was raising funds for jihad... Over the next couple of years, he says he raised $300,000... His biggest contributors? Doctors. People who were businessmen. Professional people, basically, who wanted to donate substantial amounts of money."[213]

The following conclusions are inevitable: unless the extent of retaliation on the axis of jihad nation is devastating and affects most of their population significantly, these populations have little incentive to scale down or do away with jihad.

There is a distinct possibility of the next jihadist nukes exploding in India. Pakistani newspapers have already mentioned the possibility of smuggling a device into India as a means of delivering it there.[214]

Within the next few years, India will likely see many of its strategic assets—such as oil refineries or nuclear installations—taken out by local jihadis set up and funded by Saudi Arabia and Pakistan. When this happens, for India this terror war may have reached a point of no return, with the cumulative effects of terror war and what is yet to come being equivalent to multiple nuclear strikes both in terms of lives lost and the material devastation incurred. In Kashmir and in the rest of India, jihad sponsored by Pakistan and

Saudi Arabia have already cost close to 100,000 lives in casualties and also about half a million unbelievers driven out of their land. In the years and decades ahead, if this jihad is not stopped, it is reasonable to conclude that millions will be dead and displaced, hundreds of millions more of its "infidel" children will be malnourished, which will eventually lead to an Islamic conquest of the land of India and its people. With no effective option left, in retaliation, India could hit back at both Pakistan and Saudi Arabia with strategic strikes.

There are several reasons why massive strategic strikes by India on southern and middle Saudi Arabia—away from its oil fields—and Pakistan may be appropriate. Given the genocidal nature of jihad, as discussed in *Right to Exist* Section, retaliation must be disproportionate. These strikes have the potential to deal a mortal blow to both political Islam and its dominant sponsors, as a last resort, without directly implicating America, Israel or other western powers. In other words, it is an attack by allies or semi-"proxies", similar to the kind that Saudi Arabia, Pakistan or Iran have deployed so effectively against America and its allies. The aftermath of strategic strikes would provide the American military an opportunity to "manage" Saudi oil fields in order to ensure a steady oil supply and transport.

In the public stage of the world opinion, Indian retaliation may come across as the last ditch effort by a developing secular democracy to save itself from an escalating and determined extermination. From an Indian viewpoint, Saudi Arabia and Pakistan can be portrayed as being no different than the alien civilization out to exterminate humans in the Hollywood movie *Independence*

Day, with the Saudi role akin to that played by the mother ship in this movie.

There are other reasons. Surprisingly tough Hizbollah resistance to Israel's defensive thrust into Southern Lebanon in 2006 points to the near-impossibility of conventionally defeating the armed Muslim groups embedded in civilian areas while keeping Muslim civilian casualties to a minimum. Israel will find it difficult to justify very large casualty figures among the Lebanese Muslim population, even as that population sponsors terror against Israel. Now comes the news of Hamas' military buildup in the Gaza strip— dangerously similar to Hizbollah's in Southern Lebanon—by constructing tunnels and underground bunkers and smuggling in ground-to-air missiles and military-grade explosives.[215] A promising way out for Israel is coalition building with victim nations. This would involve taking on political Islam and its fountainhead, Saudi Arabia, through a jihad-victim developing nation such as India.

Islamists see Saudi Arabia as God's nation—a holy land. Decisive strategic strikes on it will likely take away the ideological "shield" and physical "invincibility" it provides to nodes of Muslim social network. If these strikes are carried out as part of an integrated policy approach, the extent of worldwide Muslim indignance should be limited. It also sends a powerful message, for the first time, to the jihad-supporting elite—the "check writers" for jihad and lead clerics, and even the public at large in nations such as Iran, Pakistan or Saudi Arabia—that the war of thousand cuts they have imposed on unbelievers has failed. They will learn that they have a devastating price to pay, both on a personal and at the community level, should they continue.

Pope's Dilemma

As a leader of the world's dominant religion, Christianity, the Pope should be concerned. He also lives in the heart of Europe—a focused area of political Islamic assertion and demographic assault. The Pope's reference to a 14th-century Byzantine emperor's remark about Islam imposing itself found angry responses and demonstrations around the Muslim world.[216] In his November 2006 visit to Turkey, he tried to mend fences and establish a dialogue with Muslim clerics, specifically on the need for reciprocity on the part of Muslim nations to allow establishment of religious institutions for non-Muslims in Muslim lands. The Pope correctly reminded them of the scores of mosques that are being constructed in Western Europe.

But the Pope was dealing from a situation of weakness; Muslim nations are under no compulsion to be reciprocal, and he is dealing with political Islam, a conquest-driven entity. The core strategy of political Islam is to keep an iron grip on what it has conquered already while reaching out for more. The reason for the lack of reciprocity is articulated by a well-known Indian Islamist, Zakir Naik:

> In some Islamic countries propagation of other religions is prohibited. Even construction of any place of worship is also prohibited. So, many non-Muslims ask: when we allow Muslims to preach and build their mosques in our countries, then why they [non-Muslims] are not allowed to do so in these Muslim countries?... As far as matters of religion are concerned we [Muslims] know for sure that only Islam

is a True religion in the eye of God. In Quran it is mentioned that God will never accept any religion other than Islam. As far as building of Churches or Temples is concerned, how can we allow this when their religion is wrong and when their worshipping is wrong? Thus we will not allow such wrong things in our Islamic country. In religious matters only we know for sure that we Muslims are right—they [non-Muslims] are not sure. Thus in our Islamic country we can't allow preaching other religions because we know for sure that only Islam is the right religion. However, if a non-Muslim likes to practice his religion in Islamic country, then he can do so inside his home—but he can't propagate his religion. Non-Muslims are no doubt experts in science and technology. They [non- Muslims] are not sure about religious Truths. Thus we are trying to get them to the right path of Islam. Therefore we propagate our religion to the non-Muslims.[217]

The Pope may have initiated this dialogue for political reasons, by pointing out the duplicitous nature of political Islam's dealings with unbelievers. Nonetheless, there may be a downside to this: by talking with insincere Muslim clerics, the Pope may be unnecessarily giving them credibility.

The above articulation by an Indian Islamist is a typical one, showing the futility of the Pope's "dialogue". This outlook by Islamists underlines the need to discredit the ideological foundations of political Islam (Section: *Science to the Rescue*). However, many of the arguments presented in Chapter Two also cast shadow on the theological underpinnings of the Pope's own faith. Arguably, under this scenario, a Pope may never want to be part of such an ideological counter-offensive directed at political Islam. In fact, to save his own base, he could undermine such an effort. Here is the biggest irony: the faiths most threatened by political Islam, may be opposed to the most effective way of dealing with it.

Alternate Analysis

In a 2005 article, Robert Trager and Dessislava Zagorcheva have argued a case for deterring terrorism by making a case study of the apparently effective American and Philippine governments' approach to deal with Moro Islamic Liberation Front.[218]

Through repression and by emphasizing medieval Arabic way of life, political Islam has created poverty and influenced Muslims in the Philippines into embracing jihad. Aided by America, the deterrence strategy against Muslim insurgency has involved artificially increasing economic opportunities for the Muslims in the region. This approach of addressing the symptoms without adequately addressing the root cause is hardly sustainable in the long run. Based upon the data and arguments provided in Chapters Two and Three, political Islam offers little or no positive vision—and drives Muslims towards conflict with others. Importantly, it also creates conditions for Muslims to have large families, such that Muslims far surpass the growth rate of people of other denominations. All of this inherently creates an unstable situation. In some Muslim nations, repression, a form of deterrence, has been used to keep political Islam at bay. In Turkey, Mustafa Kemal Ataturk repressed political Islam; in Iraq, it was Saddam Hussein. But once the power vacuum was created in these nations, political Islam were revived. Indeed, with the advent of democracy in Turkey and the removal of Saddam, political Islam is making a comeback.

Conclusion: either containment or deterrence of radical Islam, while it can be effective in the short-term, is not effective in the long-term.

Marc Sageman argues in his book that we are facing something closer to a cult network than an organized global enemy.[219] From David Ignatius' op-ed in the *Washington Post*:

Like many cults through history, the Muslim terrorists thrive by channeling and perverting the idealism of young people. As a forensic psychiatrist, (Sageman) he analyzed data on about 400 jihadis. He found that they weren't poor, desperate sociopaths but restless young men who found identity by joining the terrorist underground. Ninety percent came from intact families; 63 percent had gone to college; 75 percent were professionals or semi-professionals; 73 percent were married.

What transformed these young Sunni Muslim men was the fellowship of the jihad and the militant role models they found in people such as Osama Bin Laden. The terrorist training camps in Afghanistan were a kind of elite finishing school—Sageman likened it to getting into Harvard. The Sept. 11 hijackers weren't psychotic killers; none of the 19 had criminal records. In terms of their psychological profiles, says

Sageman, they were as healthy as the general population.

The implication of Sageman's analysis is that the Sunni jihadism of al-Qaeda and its spin-off groups is a generational phenomenon. Unless new grievances spawn new recruits, it will gradually ebb over time. In other words, this is a fire that will gradually burn itself out unless we keep pumping in more oxygen.[220]

In this book's view, as discussed in last Chapter, the so-called grievances are mostly either self-inflicted or are even invented to spawn new jihadist recruits. In fact, the grievance strategy—contrary to what Sageman articulates—is at the core of political Islamic movement to channel Muslim energy toward conquest of unbelievers.

In a *Washington Post* op-ed *Bin Laden, The Left and Me*, which was a response to criticism of his book,[221] Dinesh D'Souza declares the American left to be partly responsible for the Muslim rage:

In my book, published this month, I argue that the American left bears a measure of responsibility for the volcano of anger from the Muslim world that produced the 9/11 attacks. President Jimmy Carter's withdrawal of support for the shah of Iran, for example, helped Ayatollah Khomeini's regime come to power in Iran, thus giving radical Islamists control of a major state; and President Bill Clinton's failure to respond to Islamic attacks confirmed Bin Laden's perceptions of U.S. weakness and emboldened him to strike on 9/11. I also argue that the policies that U.S. "progressives" promote around the world—including abortion rights, contraception for teenagers and gay rights—are viewed as an assault on traditional values by many cultures, and have contributed to the blowback of Islamic rage.

The thrust of the radical Muslim critique of America is that Islam is under attack from the global forces of atheism and immorality—and that the United States is leading that attack. This leads to the question: Why did the terrorists do it? In a 2003 statement, Bin Laden said that to him, the World Trade Center resembled the idols that the prophet Muhammad removed from Mecca. In other words, Bin Laden believes that the United States represents the pagan depravity that Muslims have a duty to resist. What would motivate Muslims in faraway countries to volunteer for martyrdom? The fact that Palestinians don't have a state? I don't think so. It's more likely that they would do it if they feared their values and way of life were threatened.[222]

The moral high-ground D'Souza gives Islamists can hardly be justified. Nations such as Saudi Arabia, Pakistan or Egypt that have a large political Islamic base have some of the highest levels of corruption anywhere in the world. As has been argued in this book, radicals had to discover and market often-unjustified "grievances" against the US in order to justify using terror. The trilogy from which extremists derive their inspiration and governance commands conquest of unbelievers; for that, unbeliever nations had to be attacked. If Muslim extremists had an alternate positive vision other than this rage, one could take D'Souza's analysis seriously. In fact, radical Muslims do not offer a positive vision, and this makes peace with them impossible to achieve.

In his 2006 book, *Overblown: How Politicians and the Terrorism Industry Inflate National Security Threats, and Why We Believe Them*, John Mueller articulates the view that the terror threat arising from Islamists is overblown.[223] He examines how hyper-vigilance regarding terrorism is threatening liberties, the economy, and lives. Mueller calls for the creation of policy that reduces fear and the cost of overreaction.

Mueller makes the mistake of not realizing that Islamic terrorism is a consequence of the ongoing conquest of land and people for political Islam. He likewise fails to recognize that terrorism is its one manifestation. Contrary to his central thesis that the political goals of terrorist movements can't succeed, we noted in the Section *Siege of India* that within the past 60 years, entire lands have been captured systematically and almost exclusively by Islam and Muslims. This process is still ongoing because of state sponsorship of these movements, notably by Saudi Arabia, Iran, Pakistan and others. Also, due to high Muslim population growth rates and due to the vast majority of Muslim populations being under political Islamic control, the terror war will only escalate in coming years. It is no longer a containable problem. What this means is America and its allies must respond now overwhelmingly (or in an overblown manner, to use Mueller's phrase) to neutralize political Islam, which is at the root of the terror and mayhem.

Reinvent America

America stands today as probably the most powerful nation ever to exist on earth. It has pulled the rest of the world along to unprecedented levels of civilizational progress. Yet it is also a caring nation, with both the government and the public generously funding schools and hospitals and giving food for the needy in developing world.

But America is also on a path of ruin due to extraordinary and escalating security-related expenses imposed by the terror war.

While Europe is under the grip of what Bruce Bawer calls "self-destructive passivity, its softness towards tyranny, its reflexive inclination to appease", America is handicapped by its holier-than-thou outlook toward religion or faith, which was shaped by the influential majority-religion lobby.[224]

This American outlook may be undercutting the most important component of a successful strategy toward winning the war on terrorism: the ability to comprehensively discredit theological or ideological foundations of political Islam.

When a political ideology uses the name of God for conquest and has proven its genocidal intent across continents, it can no longer be seen as a conventional religion or faith. Some of the arguments used to question religious foundations of political Islam—such the authenticity, accuracy or completeness of scriptures—can also pose difficulties for other faiths, including the majority religion in America. Still, the American establishment must adapt to the new enemy by using tactics that in the past would have been considered unthinkable. However, this requires an America whose leadership promotes as matter of policy, "In Science and Common Sense We Believe".

If America decides it couldn't afford to be critical of the religious basis of political Islam because this could indirectly undermine its powerful church, such an America may be rightly seen as no longer capable of making necessary adjustments to win the war on terror. History is replete with disappearing or declining civilizations that, for religious or philosophical reasons, refused to embrace a winning strategy. A surging China, which is potentially the next superpower and which is relatively free of the cost of war on terror and not particularly religious, may be best positioned to exploit the spoils.

The present popularity of books questioning the origins of religious doctrines from a scientific point of view and discussing their inconsistencies may be an indication of an American public's trying to break open the taboo of discussing religions critically.[225,226] When educated individuals acting in the name of God smash loaded airliners into city-like skyscrapers, these questions become inevitable.[227] A public and policy debate, leading to a shift toward a better appreciation of science at the expense of retrogressive religious doctrines, may be a good thing after all!

In this era, maintaining real wealth, national confidence, and even security comes down to creating and owning intellectual property in the form of patents. A 2005 innovation bipartisan study by economists Rob Shapiro and Kevin Hasset estimates that the U.S. intellectual property is worth between $5 trillion and $5.5 trillion, equivalent to about 45 percent of the GDP.[228] After peaking in the 1960s, the American share of worldwide industrial patents has reduced to about 52 percent.[229] Although globalization can be seen as contributing to this reduction, this trend also points to the need for America to remain competitive through education, training and infrastructure investments. Even as the Internet opens up America to achieve the next level of progress, the grip of religious theology can be a retarding force. A survey released by Rasmussen Reports in April 2005 found that most Americans—63 percent—believe the Bible is literally true and is the Word of God, with just 24 percent thinking otherwise.[230]

These statistics expose the weakness of American society to new knowledge and ideas. It also shows a deficiency in the American appreciation of scientific knowledge in building modern civilizations. Such a civilization doesn't attract enough of its bright students to specialize in science or engineering.

As part of the American strategy for attracting and keeping the best in America, a certain percentage of graduate enrollments in science or engineering are expected to be of foreign origin. But the data stating that at least 30 percent of graduate students in American science or engineering graduate programs were of foreign origins (the average percentage is much more—for instance, in physics the percentage was 43) may lead one to conclude that the underlying strong religious outlook reflected in the Rasmussen Report is having a negative impact on American youth.[231,232]

All of this contrasts with China or even India, where the younger generation has realized lucrative career paths by embracing science and engineering. Importantly, the majorities in these countries are not dominated by an outlook that puts emphasis on book(s) of "God's revelations" to help guide them. In an era of an increasingly information-based world, this could be a significant advantage over the theology-influenced America; the emphasis on religious information that was essentially designed for different times and conditions ultimately restricts the ability to perform in the modern world.

America was able to out-compete and bankrupt the atheist, but communist former Soviet Union because unlike America or even China, the Soviet Union never focused on wealth creation for its citizens. However, past history is no guarantee for predicting the future. The European elite, who saw themselves as the leading civilization in the early 20th century, were surprised to find that the America they had underestimated surged past them in every way during the later part of the last century. We now understand why. America embraced capitalism, while Europeans got stuck in socialism. It is conceivable that this century will likely favor those civilizations, which, in addition to capitalism, will embrace science and engineering.

If America can play the leadership role, articulating a modern vision based upon common sense and science while discrediting the roots of ideologies spawning terror, it can set forth policy decisions leading to a swift victory over political Islam and win the war on terror. America can then free up its vast resources to invest in the future of its children and in other priorities. Such an America will also reinvigorate itself to take on the strategic, scientific, technological and economic challenge posed by China.

Executive Policy Summary

Based upon the analysis and discussion in this chapter, the following summary is presented for an easy review. It outlines major elements of the dos and don'ts of a policy response going forward. (The reader is also urged to read the summary given at the beginning of this chapter.)

- o Instead of focusing on bringing democracy to Muslim-majority nations, policies should be geared toward first weakening political Islam in their societies so as to create conditions that will help to win the war on terror.
- o It is futile to talk about reformation of Islam or to hope for moderates to exercise power and influence in most Muslim societies; political Islam must first be weakened.
- o Muslim religious institutions, under the influence of political Islam, are the nodes of the social network that spawns jihad. With political Islam's power so concentrated on these nodes, these nodes are also political Islam's greatest weakness.
- o We must question and discredit the theological foundations of political Islam in order to influence educated Muslims against political Islam, thereby weakening it.
- o We must discredit the grievance basis that is used to mobilize Muslims.
- o As part of preparing the American government to wage the war effectively, it should be mandatory

for all Federal employees to take a short course on political Islam.

o Troops should be either redeployed or withdrawn from untenable situations in Iraq and Afghanistan. The so-called American troop "surge" in Iraq doesn't weaken political Islam enough to make the occupation worthwhile.

o A long-term focus on Al-Qaeda, Hizbollah, Hamas, or the Taliban is the wrong way of responding to terror. Instead, the focus should be on the sponsors—the axis of jihad, consisting of Saudi Arabia, Iran and Pakistan.

o Even leaders who are "friendly" to America in nations such as Pakistan or Saudi Arabia are prisoners of the entrenched and dominant forces of political Islam, and are largely irrelevant to the war on terror.

o It is important to discredit and distance Saudi Arabia and create to a sense of grievance regarding Saudi Arabia in the eyes of the Muslim community around the world.

o We should help to build "crimes against humanity" cases against the axis of jihad nations and to develop a sense of grievance against the axis in non-Muslim victim nations. This can be used to bring jihad-sponsoring nations into line.

o Emphasizing Iran's pre-Islamic way of life may be one way of eventually marginalizing clerics and getting them to give up reigns of power in a nation that is tired of them.

o We should rapidly help to build India as a counterforce to political Islam and axis of jihad nations, and leverage 850 million cornered Indians to fight the terror war.

From the Sections titled *Right to Exist* and *Scope for Nuclear Retaliation*:

o In America specifically, Muslim religious organizations influenced by political Islam should be neutralized on the grounds of being hostile to America and on the grounds of right of preemption. This includes even those that do not appear to be threatening at this time.

o With the above step as an example, help to break the back of political Islam in nations with minority Muslim populations, paving the way for liberation of Muslims from political Islam.

o In order to comprehensively remove political Islam's ability to wage a never-ending and asymmetric war of genocide, unbeliever nations have the right, at times, to respond in a disproportionate way, using every means possible.

o Develop an allied nuclear retaliation strategy outlining a scope for preemptive and devastating strategic strikes on nations sponsoring jihad.

Notes

1. Rudi Williams, "Terror War 'Inescapable Calling of Our Generation,' Bush Says," *American Forces Press Service, March 20, 2004,* http://www.defenselink.mil/news/ /newsarticle.aspx?id=27028.

What Went Wrong?

2. John Lehman, "We're Not Winning This War," *The Washington Post,* August 31, 2006, http://www. washingtonpost.com/wp-dyn/content/article/2006/ 08/30/AR2006083002730.html.

3. Harlan Ullman, "Divided 'They' Fall," *The Washington Times,* April 4, 2007, http://www.washingtontimes.com/ op-ed/hullman.htm.

4. "Rising Price of the War on Terror," *Christian Science Monitor,* November 21, 2006, http://www.csmonitor.com/ 2006/1121/p01s03-usmi.html.

5. William Warner, "The Study of Political Islam," *FrontPage Magazine,* February 5, 2007, http://www.frontpagemag. com/Articles/ReadArticle.asp?ID=26769.

6. Mary Habeck, *Knowing the Enemy: Jihadist Ideology and the War on Terror* (Yale University Press, 2006), p. 42-43.

7. Rachel Ehrenfeld, "Saudi Dollars and Jihad," *FrontPage Magazine,* October 24, 2005, http://www.frontpagemag. com/Articles/ReadArticle.asp?ID=19938.

8. Shine Dighe and Charisma Murari, "The Life and Times of HEH," *The Times of India,* July 3, 2006, http:// timesofindia.Indiatimes.com/articleshow/msid-1702680, prtpage-1.cms.

9. Steven Stalinsky, "Saudi Arabia's Education System," *FrontPage Magazine*, December 30, 2002, http://www. frontpagemag.com/Articles/ReadArticle.asp?ID=5243.

10. Arnaud de Borchgrave, "Pakistan, Saudi Arabia in Secret Nuke Pact," *The Washington Times*, October 22, 2003, http://www.washtimes.com/world/20031021-112804-8451r.htm.

11. Arnie Schifferdecker, "The Taliban-Bin Laden-ISI Connection," *American Foreign Service Association*, December 1, 2002, http://www.afsa.org/fsj/Dec01/schiff.cfm.

12. Lawrence Right, The *Looming Tower: Al-Qaeda and the Road to 9/11* (Alfred A. Knopf, 2006), p. 291.

13. Condoleezza Rice, *National Commission on Terrorist Attacks upon the United States, Ninth Public Hearing*, April 8, 2004, http://www.9-11c omission.gov/archive/hearing9/9-11CommissionHearing_2004-04-08.htm.

14. Gary Berntsen, *Jawbreaker: The Attack on Bin Laden and Al Qaeda: A Personal Account by the CIA's Key Field Commander* (Crown, 2005).

15. Mathew Levitt, "The Political Economy of Middle East Terrorism," *Middle East Review of International Affairs*, December, 2002, http://meria.idc.ac.il/journal/2002/issue4/jv6n4a3.html.

16. John Burns, "How Afghan's Stern Rulers Took Hold," *The New York Times*, 1996.

17. Peter Bergen, "Afghanistan Testimony Before the House Committee on Foreign Affairs," *New American Foundation*, April 7, 2007. http://www.newamerica.net/publications/resources/2007/peter_bergens_afghanistan_testimony_before_the_house_committee_on_

foreign_affairs.

18. Aryn Baker, "A Taliban Spokesman's Confession," *Time*, January 17, 2007, http://www.time.com/time/world/article /0,8599,1579979,00.html.

19. Ahmed Rashid, "Accept Defeat by Taliban, Pakistan Tells NATO," *Telegraph*, November 30, 2006, http://www. Telegraph.co.uk/news/main.jhtml?xml=/news/2006/11/29/ wafghan29.xml.

20. Brian Eads, "Saudi Arabia's Deadly Export," *Australian Reader's Digest,* February 2003, p. 119-125.

21. Ted Carpenter, "Terrorist Sponsors: Saudi Arabia, Pakistan, China," *Cato Institute*, November 16, 2001, http://www.cato.org/pub_display.php?pub_id=3841.

22. Stephen Schwartz, "Ground Zero and the Saudi Connection," *The Spectator*, September 22, 2001.

23. Rachel Ehrenfeld, "The Cure for the Wahhabi Virus," *FrontPage Magazine*, October 24, 2005, http://www. frontpagemag.com/Articles/ReadArticle.asp?ID=19853.

24. "The Great Divide: How Westerners and Muslims View Each Other," *Pew Global Attitudes Poll,* June 22, 2006, http://pewglobal.org/reports/display.php?ReportID= 253.

25. Steven Emerson, *National Commission on Terrorist Attacks Upon the United States, Third Public Hearing*, July 9, 2003, http://www.9-11commission.gov/hearings/ hearing3/witness_emerson.htm.

26. S. Balakrishnan, "Attacks Retaliation for Gujarat Riots?," *The Times of India*, July 13, 2006, http://timesofindia. Indiatimes.com/articleshow/1742854.cms.

27. Richard Halloran, "SEA Terror," *The Washington Times*, April 21, 2007, http://www.washingtontimes.com/commentary/20070420-080426-8307r.htm.

28. R. Upadhyay, "Islamic Terrorism in Bangladesh – A Threat to Regional Peace," *SAAG.org*, May 10, 2007, http://www.saag.org/papers23/paper2242.html.

29. Daniel Byman, *Deadly Connections: States That Sponsor Terrorism* (Cambridge University Press, 2007).

30. "Hizballah Rockets," *GlobalSecurity.org*, http://www.globalsecurity.org/military/world/para/hizballah-rockets.htm.

31. Daniel Byman, *Deadly Connections: States That Sponsor Terrorism* (Cambridge University Press, 2007), p. 156.

32. "Kashmir Militant Extremists," *Council on Foreign relations*, July 12, 2006, http://www.cfr.org/publication/9135.

33. Hamid Mir, "'We can Hit any Soft Target in India'," *Rediff.com*, January 9, 2007, http://ushome.rediff.com/news/2007/jan/09inter.htm.

34. B. Raman, "India & Pakistan: Can Mindsets & Perceptions Change?" *SAAG.org*, December 10, 2006, http://www.saag.org/papers21/paper2057.html.

35. Krishnakumar, "A Silent Genocide is Taking Place in Bangladesh," *Rediff.com*, November 21, 2006, http://www.rediff.com/news/2006/nov/21rights.htm.

36. Annexure, *Hamoodur Rahman Commission Report*, July 1972, http://www.bangla2000.com/bangladesh/Independence-War/Report-Hamoodur-Rahman/Annexure.shtm.

37. Mashuqur Rahman, "The Demons of 1971," *Rediff.com*, January 4, 2007, http://www.rediff.com/news/2007/jan/

04spec.htm.

38. Bob Woodward, *State of Denial: Bush at War, Part III* (Simon & Shuster, 2006).

39. Philippe Girard, *Paradise Lost: Haiti's Tumultuous Journey from Pearl of the Caribbean to Third World Hotspot* (Palgrave MacMillan, 2005).

40. Edward Luttwak, "Dead End: Counterinsurgency Warfare as Military Malpractice," *Harper's Magazine*, March 5, 2007.

41. Moorthy Muthuswamy, "Bring Democracy to Iraq," *The Washington Times*, July 19, 2003.

42. Moorthy Muthuswamy, "Pakistan's Undemocratic Underpinnings," *The Washington Times*, November 22, 2002.

43. Moorthy Muthuswamy, "A New Paradigm for the War on Terror," *The Washington Times*, December 8, 2003.

44. Joshua Hammer, "Freedom is Not Enough," *Newsweek*, November 14, 2005.

45. Lydia Polgreen, "Africa's Crisis of Democracy," *The New York Times*, April 23, 2007.

46. "Freedom in the World - China (2006)," *Freedom House*, http://www.freedomhouse.org/inc/content/pubs/fiw/ inc_country_detail.cfm?year=2006&country=6941&pf.

47. Fareed Zakaria, "India Rising," *Newsweek*, March 2, 2006, http://www.msnbc.msn.com/id/11564364/site/ newsweek.

48. Fareed Zakaria, *The Future of Freedom: Illiberal Democracy at Home and Abroad* (W. W. Norton & Company, 2003), p. 154.

49. Bill Spindle, "Crude Reality: Soaring Energy Use Puts Oil Squeeze on Iran," *The Wall Street Journal*, February 20, 2007.

50. Andrew Bostom, "The 9/11 Commission and Jihad," *FrontPage Magazine*, July 30, 2004, http://www. frontpagemag.com/Articles/ReadArticle.asp?ID=14439.

51. Chapter 12, *National Commission on Terrorist Attacks upon the United States*, http://www.9-11commission. gov/report/911Report_Ch12.htm.

Passion for Conquest

52. Bernard Lewis, *The Crisis of Islam* (Thorndike Press, 2003).

53. Ali Sina, "Yes, Study the Quran!" *FaithFreedom.org*, January 21, 2004, http://www.faithfreedom.org/oped/ sina40121.htm.

54. Robert Spencer, *The Truth About Muhammad: Founder of the World's Most Intolerant Religion* (Regnery, 2006).

55. The Islamic Trilogy: Volume 3, *A Simple Koran: Readable and Understandable* (Center for the Study of Political Islam, 2006), p. 395.

56. Mary Habeck, *Knowing the Enemy: Jihadist Ideology and the War on Terror* (Yale University Press, 2006), p. 17.

57. Andrew Bostom, "Confused Islamic Apologetics," *FrontPage Magazine*, August 10, 2004, http://www. frontpagemag.com/Articles/ReadArticle.asp?ID=14578.

58. William Warner, "An Ethical Basis for the War Against Political Islam," *Center for the Study of Political Islam*, 2006, p. 13.

59. Mary Habeck, *Knowing the Enemy: Jihadist Ideology and the War on Terror* (Yale University Press, 2006), p. 20-22.

60. Mary Habeck, *Knowing the Enemy: Jihadist Ideology and the War on Terror* (Yale University Press, 2006), p. 24.

61. Mary Habeck, *Knowing the Enemy: Jihadist Ideology and the War on Terror* (Yale University Press, 2006), p. 6-7.

62. Mary Habeck, *Knowing the Enemy: Jihadist Ideology and the War on Terror* (Yale University Press, 2006), p. 28-29.

63. RSS Feeds, "Pakistan Mosques to Preach Family Planning", *The Times of India*, December 18, 2006, http://timesofindia.indiatimes.com/NEWS/World/ Pakistan/Mosques_in_Pakistan_to_preach_family_planning /articleshow/839925.cms.

64. Moorthy Muthuswamy, "Certain Koran Verses Threaten World Safety," *The Washington Times*, October 2, 2001.

65. The Islamic Trilogy: Volume 2, *The Political Traditions of Mohammed: The Hadith for the Unbelievers* (Center for the Study of Political Islam, 2006), p. 143.

66. The Islamic Trilogy: Volume 2, *The Political Traditions of Mohammed: The Hadith for the Unbelievers* (Center for the Study of Political Islam, 2006), p. 144.

67. The Islamic Trilogy: Volume 1, *Mohammed and the Unbelievers: A Political Life* (Center for the Study of Political Islam, 2006), p. 126.

68. Asra Nomani, "Islam and Women: Clothes Aren't the Issue," *The Washington Post*, October 22, 2006, http://www.washingtonpost.com/wp-dyn/content/article /2006/10/20/AR2006102001261.html.

Many a Face of Jihad

69. The Islamic Trilogy: Volume 1, *Mohammed and the Unbelievers: A Political Life* (Center for the Study of Political Islam, 2006), p. 164-165.

70. Efraim Karsh, *Islamic Imperialism : A History* (Yale University Press, 2006).

71. Michael Kinsley, "It's Not Apartheid: Carter Adds to the List of Mideast Misjudgments," *The Washington Post*, December 12, 2006, http://www.washingtonpost.com/wp-dyn/content/article/2006/12/11/AR2006121101225. html?nav=rss_opinion/.

72. Daniel Goldhagen, "A Manifesto for Murder," *The Los Angeles Times*, February 5, 2006.

73. Bruce Bawer, *While Europe Slept: How Radical Islam is Destroying the West from Within* (Doubleday, 2006), p. 32-33.

74. "CIA – The World Factbook - Netherlands," 2006, https://www.cia.gov/cia/publications/factbook/geos/nl.html.

75. Bruce Bawer, *While Europe Slept: How Radical Islam is Destroying the West from Within* (Doubleday, 2006), p. 236.

76. Daniel Pipes, "More Survey Research from a British Islamist Hell," July 26, 2005, http://www.danielpipes.org/blog/483.

77. Daniel Allott, "Islam and Violence," *The Washington Times*, December 4, 2006, http://www.washtimes.com/op-ed/20061203-100623-9818r.htm.

78. Mark Steyn, "Who Will Raise the Siege of Paris?," *The Washington Times*, November 7, 2005, http://www.washingtontimes.com/commentary/20051106-102157

-9880r.htm.

79. Graeme Wilson, "Young, British Muslims 'Getting More Radical'," *Telegraph*, March 1, 2007, http://www. telegraph.co.uk/news/main.jhtml?xml=/news/2007/01/29/ nmuslims29.xml.

80. Hasan Suroor, "A Question of Identity," *The Hindu*, August 17, 2004, http://www.hindu.com/2004/08/17/ stories/2004081701341000.htm.

81. Amit Roy, "7/7 Report Links Bombers to Pak," *The Telegraph*, May 11, 2006, http://www.telegraphindia. com/1060512/asp/foreign/story_6214208.asp.

82. Bruce Bawer, *While Europe Slept: How Radical Islam is Destroying the West from Within* (Doubleday, 2006), p. 30.

83. Bruce Bawer, *While Europe Slept: How Radical Islam is Destroying the West from Within* (Doubleday, 2006), p. 41-42.

84. Paul Belien, "Islamicization of Antwerp," *The Washington Times*, March 14, 2007, http://www.washingtontimes.com/ op-ed/20070313-090315-9588r.htm.

85. Moorthy Muthuswamy, "Why the EU does not Want Turkey," *The Washington Times*, December 18, 2002.

86. Paul Belien, "In bed with Islamists," *The Washington Times*, April 11, 2007, http://www.washingtontimes. com/op-ed/20070410-100624-4394r.htm.

87. K. Lal, *The Legacy of Muslim Rule in India* (Voice of India, New Delhi).

88. Koenraad Elst, *Negationism in India: Concealing the Record of Islam* (Voice of India, 1992), http:// koenraadelst.bharatvani.org/books/negaind/index.htm.

89. Balbir Punj, "Hindu-Muslim Dishonesty," *Organiser,* May 22, 2006, http://www.organiser.org/dynamic/ modules.php?name=Content&pa=showpage&pid=79& page=9.

90. K. Phanda, "Balkanising India," *The Pioneer,* April 14, 2006.

91. "Indian Muslim Nationalism," *Wikipedia,* http://en. wikipedia.org/wiki/Indian_Muslim_nationalism.

92. S. Bhattacharyya, *Genocide in East Pakistan/Bangladesh* (A. Ghosh, 1987), Preface.

93. "Hindus in Bangladesh, Pakistan and Kashmir: A Survey of Human Rights," *Hindu American Foundation,* 2004, http://www.hinduamericanfoundation.org/HHR2004. pdf.

94. "CIA – The World Factbook - Pakistan," 2006, https://www .cia.gov/cia/publications/factbook/geos/pk.html.

95. "Muslim population growth in India," *Wikipedi,* http://en. wikipedia.org/wiki/Muslim_population_growth_in_India.

96. Jehangir Pocha, "India Erecting a Barrier Along Bangladesh Border," *The Boston Globe,* May 30, 2004, http://www.boston.com/news/world/articles/2004/05/ 30/india_erecting_a_barrier_along_bangladesh_border/.

97. Subramanian Swamy, "A Strategy to Combat Terrorism in India," *Organiser,* October 8, 2006,http://www.organiser. org/dynamic/modules.php?name=Content&pa=showpage &pid=151&page=25; Also, from a note published by the Author.

98. From the pages of Pakistani English language dailies (1999-200).

99. APP, "Musharraf for Developing Knowledge-based Economy," *The Daily Times,* November 19, 2006, http://www.dailytimes.com.pk/default.asp?page=2006 \11\19\story_19-11-2006_pg13_1.

100."Education in Post-Independence India: Some Milestones," http://www.education.nic.in/sector.asp #milestone.

101.Maloy Dhar, *Fulcrum of Evil : ISI, CIA, Al Qaeda Nexus* (Manas, 2006).

102.RSS feeds, "*LeT* Terrorists kill 22 Hindus in Kashmir," *The Times of India*, May 1, 2006,http://timesofindia. indiatimes.com/articleshow/1511180.cms.

103.Qudssia Akhlaque, "Dialogue to start next month: Joint Statement on Musharraf -Vajpayee meeting," *Dawn*, January 7, 2004, http://www.dawn.com/2004/01/07/top1. Htm.

104.Staff Reporter, "No Pakistani to be Handed Over to India," *Dawn*, January 13, 2002, http://www.dawn.com/ 2004/01/07/top1.htm.

105.Jagmohan, *My Frozen Turbulence in Kashmir* (Allied, 2002), p. 180.

106."Kashmir Region," *Wikipedia,* http://en.wikipedia.org/ wiki/Kashmir.

107.Sunil Fotedar et. al., "Living Under the Shadow of Article 370," *The Kashmir Herald*, January 1, 2002, http:// kashmirherald.com/featuredarticle/article370.html.

108.Arvind Lavakare, "The Woes of Jammu and Ladakh," *Rediff.com*, July 17, 2002, http://www.rediff.com/news/ 2002/jul/17arvind.htm.

109. Rajeev Srinivasan, "India, the Kashmiri Colony," *Rediff.com*, November 9, 2002, http://www.rediff.com/news/2002/nov/09rajeev.htm.

110. Surinder Oberoi, "Ethnic Separatism and Insurgency in Kashmir," *Asia Pacific Center for Security Studies*, http://www.apcss.org/Publications/Edited%20Volumes/ReligiousRadicalism/PagesfromReligiousRadicalism andSecurityinSouthAsiach8.pdf.

111. Mukhtar Ahmad, "J&K Assembly Passes Shariat Bill," *Rediff.com*, February 9, 2007, http://www.rediff.com/news/2007/feb/09mukhtar.htm.

112. Maloy Dhar, *Fulcrum of Evil: ISI, CIA, Al-Qaeda Nexus* (Manas, 2006), p. 185.

113. Aakar Patel, "Where Indian Muslims have Gone Wrong?," *Mid-Day*, September 5, 2004, http://ww1.mid-day.com/news/city/2004/september/91708.htm.

114. R. Upadhyay, "Islamic Institutions in India - Protracted Movement for Separate Muslim Identity?," *SAAG.org*, February 6, 2003, http://www.saag.org/papers6/paper599.html.

115. Staff Reporter, "Bush: India a Jobs Opportunity, not an Obstacle," *AP*, March 3, 2006, http://www.msnbc.msn.com/id/11650277/.

116. Fareed Zakaria, *The Future of Freedom: Illiberal Democracy at Home and Abroad* (W. W. Norton & Company, 2003), p. 145.

117. Suman Mozumder, "India Occupying Kashmir, says *Newsweek*'s Zakaria," *Rediff.com*, June 25, 2001, http://www.rediff.com/us/2001/jun/25us6.htm/.

118. Moorthy Muthuswamy, "Pakistan and Militant Islam," *The Washington Times*, September 25, 2004, http://www.washingtontimes.com/op-ed/20040925-102813-2898r.htm.

119. Fareed Zakaria, "Vengeance of the Victors," *Newsweek*, January 8, 2007, http://www.msnbc.msn.com/id/16409404/site/newsweek/.

120. PTI, "ISI Fomenting Trouble in India's North-east: US Intelligence," *Rediff.com*, April 23, 2006, http://www.rediff.com/news/2007/apr/23isi.htm.

121. Moorthy Muthuswamy, "New Ideas for a New War," *Sulekha*, April 2, 2003, http://news.sulekha.com/newsanalysisdisplay.aspx?cid=2651.

122. Commentary, "Terrorists & Politicians," *Newsinsight.net*, March 9, 2006, http://www.newsinsight.net/archivedebates/nat2.asp?recno=1349&ctg=politics.

123. Manjari Mishra, "Produce Babies, Get Reward," *The Times of India*, January 23, 2007, http://timesofindia.indiatimes.com/articleshow/1386975.cms.

124. C. Issac, "For Hindus in Kerala it's Now or Never," *Organiser*, October 32, 2004, http://www.hvk.org/articles/1104/25.html.

125. PTI, "Bukhari Meets PM, Demands Economic Package, Reservation," April 18, 2006, http://www.outlookindia.com/pti_news.asp?id=378727.

126. Omar Khalidi, *Khaki and the Ethnic Violence in India* (Three Essays Collective, 2003).

127. Balbir Punj, "The Two-Regiment Theory," *The Outlook*, March 20, 2006.

128.Omar Khalidi, *Muslims in Indian Economy* (Three Essays Collective, 2006).

129."Census India 2001," http://www.censusindia.net/results/2001census_data_index.html.

130.O. Gupta, "Hindu Youth Reduced to Second-Class Status," *Organiser*, March 25, 2007, http://www.Organizer.org/dynamic/modules.php?name=Content&pa =showpage&pid=176&page=3.

131."New Survey Busts Sachar Panel Report," *ibnlive.com*, April 6 , 2007, http://www.ibnlive.com/news/new-survey-busts-sachar-panel-report/top/37856-3.html?xml.

132.Sunil Jain, "Sachar Report: Myth and Reality," *Rediff.com*, December 11, 2006, http://www. rediff.com/news/2006/dec/11sachar.htm?zcc=rl.

133.Peter Wonacott, "Lawless Legislators Thwart Social Progress in India," *The Wall Street Journal*, May 4, 2007.

134.B. Raman, "National Security: My Jaipur Musings," *SAAG.org*, February 6, 2007, http://www.saag.org/%5Cpapers22%5Cpaper2123.html.

135.PTI, "Sachar Report to be Implemented in Full: Minister," *Rediff.com*, December 28, 2006, http://www. rediff.com/news/2006/dec/28sachar.htm?zcc=rl.

136.Balbir Punj, "Realpolitik: In Defence of the Rashtriya Suraksha Yatra," *Organiser*, April 2, 2006, http://www. organiser.org/dynamic/modules.php?name=Content&pa= showpage&pid=124&page=7.

137.PTI, "'Muslims Must have First Claim on Resources'," *The Indian Express*, December 9, 2006, http://www. expressindia.com/fullstory.php?newsid=77972.

138.Editorial, "Congress Communal Campaign," *Organiser*, April 29, 2007, http://www.organiser.org/dynamic/

modules.php?name=Content&pa=showpage&pid=
181&page=7.

139."2002 Gujarat Violence," Wikipedia, http://en.wikipedia.
org/wiki/2002_Gujarat_violence.

140.The Hindu literacy percentage in India is very similar to
the overall national average; "CIA – The World Factbook -
India," 2006, https://www.cia.gov/cia/publications/
factbook/geos/in.html.

141.Andy Mukherjee, "Commentary: India's Fiscal Advance,
Sadly, is an Illusion," *IHT*, June 3, 2005, http://www.
iht.com/articles/2005/06/02/bloomberg/sxmuk.php.

142.Harish Khare, "Manmohan Seeks $150 Billion U.S.
Investment," *The Hindu*, September 23, 2004,
http://www.hindu.com/2004/09/23/stories/
2004092308921101.htm.

143.Sultan Shahin, "Manmohan's Kashmir Dreams," *The Asia
Times Online,* November 14, 2004, http://www.atimes.
com/atimes/South_Asia/FK19Df02.html.

144.George Iype, "Why Chidambaram Hiked Defense Outlay,"
Rediff.com, July 9, 2004, http://ia.rediff.com/news/2004/
jul/09spec1.htm.

145.Swapan Dasgupta, "Asia's Other Maoist Threat," *The
Daily Times*, April 25, 2006, http://www.dailytimes.com.
pk/default.asp?page=2006%5C04%5C25%5Cstory_25-4-
2006_pg4_22.

146.PTI, "Naxalism Single Biggest Internal Security
Challenge: PM," *Rediff.com*, April 13, 2006, http://www.
rediff.com/news/2006/apr/13naxal.htm.

147."Could these Candidates be Lawmakers?,"
Indiatogether.com, May, 2004, http://www.

indiatogether.org/2004/may/gov-karpolls.htm.

148. Agencies, "Natwar's Tirade: Steps Up Attack on PM," *The Central Chronicle*, August 10, 2006, http://www.centralchronicle.com/20060810/1008001.htm.

149. Ramesh Kandula, "Terrorism Most Dangerous Threat, Says Manmohan," *The Tribune*, October 26, 2006, http://www.tribuneindia.com/2006/20061027/main1.htm.

150. Commentary, "Seal His Lips," *Newinsight.net*, April 7, 2007, http://www.newsinsight.net/archivedebates/nat2.asp?recno=1560.

151. "10 Questions: What About Pakistan?," *Stimson.org*, March 2, 2007, http://www.stimson.org/pub.cfm?id=401.

152. Moorthy Muthuswamy, "Talks with Pakistan: Overcoming Prithiviraj Syndrome," *SAAG.org*, January 23, 2004, http://www.saag.org/papers10/paper901.html.

Policy Response

153. Fareed Zakaria, *The Future of Freedom: Illiberal Democracy at Home and Abroad* (W. W. Norton & Company, 2003), p. 135.

154. Richard Rahn, "Economic liberty and Islam," *The Washington Times*, March 5, 2007, http://www.washingtontimes.com/commentary/20070304-094010-8712r.htm.

155. "Universal Declaration of Human Rights," *The UN Charter*, December 10, 1948, http://www.un.org/Overview/rights.html.

156. Sarah Downey, "A Safe Heaven," *Newsweek*, September 30, 2002, http://www.hvk.org/articles/1002/69.html.

157. Fareed Zakaria, *The Future of Freedom: Illiberal Democracy at Home and Abroad* (W. W. Norton & Company, 2003), p. 150.

158. Reza Aslan, *No god but God: The Origins, Evolution, and Future of Islam* (Random House, 2005).

159. Geneive Abdo, "A More Islamic Islam," *The Washington Post*, March 17, 2007, http://www.washingtonpost.com/wp-dyn/content/article/2007/03/16/AR2007031601941.html.

160. "Undercover Mosque," *Dispatches*, January 15, 2007, http://www.channel4.com/news/articles/dispatches/underc over+mosque/158390.

161. Jackson Nyamuya Maogoto, *Battling Terrorism: Legal Perspectives On The Use Of Force And The War On Terror* (Ashgate, 2005), p. 152.

162. Moorthy Muthuswamy, "Waffling on Islamic Ideology," *The Washington Times*, December 8, 2002.

163. Zahid Hussain, *Frontline Pakistan: The Struggle With Militant Islam* (Columbia University Press, 2007).

164. Ahmed Rashid, "Musharraf at the Exit," *The Washington Post*, March 22, 2007, http://www.washingtonpost.com/wp-dyn/content/article/2007/03/21/AR2007032101786.html.

165. Mark Steyn, *America Alone: The End of the World as We Know It* (Regnery, 2006), p. 208.

166. Moorthy Muthuswamy, "Religious Apartheid in India and American Policy Response," *Ivarta.com*, July 4, 2005, http://www.ivarta.com/columns/OL_050704.htm.

167. Helene Cooper, "Unfriendly Views on U.S.-Backed Arabic TV," *The New York Times*, May 17, 2007.

168. David Kilcullen, "'Twenty-Eight Articles': Fundamentals of Company-level Counterinsurgency," *Military Review*, May 1, 2006.

169. Jagmohan, *My Frozen Turbulence in Kashmir* (Allied, 2002), p. 401.

170. B. Raman, "Waziristanisation of Southern Thailand - International Terrorism Monitor," *SAAG.org*, February 22, 2007, http://www.saag.org/%5Cpapers22%5 Cpaper2148.html.

171. David Sanger, "Bush Adds Troops in Bid to Secure Iraq," *The New York Times*, January 10, 2007.

172. "The Iraq Study Group Report," http://bakerinstitute .org/Pubs/iraqstudygroup_findings.pdf.

173. Carl Conetta, "Resolving Iraq: Progress Depends on a Short Timeline for US Troop Withdrawal", *Project on Defense Alternatives Briefing Memo #40*, January 18, 2007, http://www.comw.org/pda/0701bm40.html.

174. AP, "Saudis reportedly funding Iraqi Sunni insurgents," *Usatoday*, December 8, 2006, http://www.usatoday.com/ news/world/iraq/2006-12-08-saudis-sunnis_x.htm.

175. Elise Labott, "Official: Saudis to Back Sunnis if U.S. Leaves Iraq," *CNN*, December 13, 2006, http://www.cnn.com/ 2006/WORLD/meast/12/13/saudi.sunnis/index.html.

176. Mark Thompson, "Where are the New Recruits?," *Time*, January 10, 2005, http://www.time.com/time/magazine/ article/0,9171,1015898,00.html.

177. Pazir Gul, "Waziristan Accord Signed," *Dawn*, September 6, 2006, http://www.dawn.com/2006/09/06/top2.htm.

178. "Declaration of the Causes and Necessity of Taking up Arms," July 6, 1775, http://odur.let.rug.nl/~usa/D/ 1751-1775/war/causes.htm.

179. Bob Woodward, *State of Denial: Bush at War, Part III* (Simon & Shuster, 2006), p. 76.

180. Vali Nasr and Ray Takeyh, "The Iran Option That isn't on the Table," *The Washington post*, February 8, 2006, http://www.washingtonpost.com/wp-dyn/content/article/2007/02/07/AR2007020702136.html.

181. Arnaud Borchgrave, "'Long War,' Not WW IV," *The Washington Times*, February 28, 2007, http://www.washtimes.com/commentary/20070227-084731-6067r.htm.

182. Roya Hakakian, "Persian . . . or Iranian?," *The Wall Street Journal*, December 28, 2006.

183. Ilan Berman, "Detente with Tehran?," *The Washington Times*, April 9, 2007, http://www.washingtontimes.com/op-ed/20070408-101851-9786r.htm.

184. "Hate Crime Laws," *Anti-defamation League*, http://www.adl.org/99hatecrime/intro.asp.

185. Joe Wolverton, "Are You the Enemy?," *The New American*, October 30, 2006, http://www.jbs.org/node/1782.

186. Josh Mancester, "Why Newt is Right," *TCS Daily*, December 5, 2006, http://www.tcsdaily.com/article.aspx?id=120506B.

187. Warren Hoge, "Dismay Over New U.N. Human Rights Council," *The New York Times*, March 11, 2007.

188. Daniel Pipes, *Next Steps in Israeli-Palestinian Peace Process: Hearing of the Subcommittee on the Middle East and South Asia of the House Foreign Affairs Committee*, February 14, 2007, http://www.danielpipes.org/article/4322.

189."International Crimes," http://www.international crimes.com/war.htm.

190.Sridhar Krishnaswami, "Pak admits Having Helped Insurgency in J&K," *Rediff.com*, October 6, 2006, http://www.rediff.com/news/2006/oct/06pak.htm.

191.R. Hariharan, "War Against Terror: ICJ Ruling on State's Role in Genocide," *SAAG.org*, March 11, 2007, http://www.saag.org/papers22/paper2163.html.

192.Iftikar Gilani, "Saudi Arabia, India Fail to Sign Anti-terror Accord," *The Daily Times*, January 27, 2006, http://www.dailytimes.com.pk/default.asp?page= 2006%5C01%5C27%5Cstory_27-1-2006_pg7_46.

193.Bhabani Dikshit, "Free Flow of Funds Sustains Terrorism," *The Daily Excelsior*, April 17, 2002, http://www.dailyexcelsior.com/02apr17/edit.htm#3.

194.Subhash Kapila, "South Asia's Conflict Generation and its External Inputs," *SAAG.org*, November 22, 2004, http://www.saag.org/papers12/paper1170.html.

195.Selig Harrison, "Pressuring Pakistan to Curb the Taliban," *The Boston Globe*, February 19, 2007, http://www.boston.com/news/globe/editorial_opinion/oped /articles/2007/02/19/pressuring_pakistan_to_curb_the_ taliban/.

196.Moorthy Muthuswamy, "Pakistan's 'Irrational Jihad Factory' a Threat to Global Stability," *The Washington Times*, July 18, 2001.

197.Symposium, "The First Nuclear Terrorist Power," *FrontPage Magazine*, March 23, 2007, http://www. frontpagemag.com/Articles/ReadArticle.asp?ID=27517.

198."Implemetation of 9/11 Commission Recommendations Act of 2007," *Americanprogress.org*, http://www.american

progress.org/issues/2007/01/securing_america.html.

199.Stephen Schwartz, "The Saudi Arabia Accountability Act of 2005," *The Weekly Standard*, June 8, 2005, http://www. weeklystandard.com/Content/Public/Articles/000/000/005/ 703azlsf.asp.

200.Stefan Halper, "Generals Dodge a Bullet on Iraq war," *The Washington Times*, April 23, 2007, http://www. washingtontimes.com/commentary/20070422-110538-9555r.htm.

201.Gurcharan Das, "The India Model," *Foreign Affairs*, July/August, 2006.

202.Narendra Modi was rated either as the most admired or as the most able chief minister in India in at least two polls.

203.Moorthy Muthuswamy, "Jihadist Threat in India," *The Washington Times*, December 21, 2006.

204.Pam Fessler, "DHS Seeks Radiation-Sensing Gear Despite Critics," *PBS*, April 17, 2007, http://www.npr.org/ templates/story/story.php?storyId=9626755.

205.William Broad, "Eye on Iran, Rivals Pursuing Nuclear Power," *The New York Times*, April 15, 2007.

206.Akaki Dvali, "Will Saudi Arabia Acquire Nuclear Weapons?" *Monterey Institute of International Studies*, March 2004, http://www.nti.org/e_research/e3_40a.html.

207.James Zumwalt, "Nuke Forsenics: No 'Cold Cases'," *The Washington Times*, March 8, 2007, http://www. washtimes.com/commentary/20070307-091631-2252r.htm.

208.K. Parthasarathy, "Health Effects at Hiroshima, Nagasaki," *The Hindu*, September 6, 2001, http://www.

hindu.com/thehindu/2001/09/06/stories/08060003.htm.

209. Noah Feldman, "Weighing the Threat of an Islamic A-Bomb," *International Herald tribune*, October 28-29, 2006.

210. Craig Smith, "Finally, I agree with Kerry on Something!," *The WorldNetdaily*, November 5, 2004, http://www.wnd.com/news/article.asp?ARTICLE_ID=41314.

211. "CIA – The World Factbook – Saudi Arabia," 2006, https://www.cia.gov/cia/publications/factbook/geos/sa.html.

212. Elaine Sciolino, "Our Saudi Allies," *The New York Times*, January 27, 2002.

213. Bob Simon, "Killing in the Name of Islam is a Cancer," *CBSNEWS*, March 27, 2005, http://www.cbsnews.com/stories/2007/03/23/60minutes/main2602308_page2.shtml.

214. This was noted in a Pakistani English language daily between the years 1998-2004.

215. Steven Erlanger, "Israel Warns of Hamas Military Buildup in Gaza," *The New York Times*, April 1, 2007.

216. Charles Krauthammer, "Tolerance: A Two-Way Street, "*The Washington Post*, September 22, 2006, http://www.washingtonpost.com/wp-dyn/content/article/2006/09/21/AR2006092101513.html.

217. "Thus Spake Dr. Zakir Naik," http://groups.google.to/group/soc.culture.pakistan/msg/431f6988e7683ee5.

218. Robert Trager et. al., *Deterring Terrorism: It Can Be Done*, International Security - Volume 30, Number 3, 2005/06, p. 87-123.

219. Marc Sageman, *Understanding Terror Networks* (University of Pennsylvania Press, 2004).

220. David Ignatius, "Young Anger Foments Jihad," *The Washington Post*, September 6, 2006, http://www.washingtonpost.com/wp-dyn/content/article/2006/09/12/AR2006091201298.html.

221. Dinesh D'Souza, *The Enemy At Home: The Cultural Left and Its Responsibility for 9/11* (Doubleday, 2007).

222. Dinesh D'Souza, "Bin Laden, the Left and Me," *The Washington Post*, January 28, 2007, http://www.washingtonpost.com/wp-dyn/content/article/2007/01/26/AR2007012601624.html.

223. John Mueller, *Overblown: How Politicians and the Terrorism Industry Inflate National Security Threats, and Why We Believe Them* (Free Press, 2006).

224. Bruce Bawer, *While Europe Slept: How Radical Islam is Destroying the West from Within* (Doubleday, 2006), p. 233.

225. Sam Harris, *Letter to a Christian Nation* (Knopf, 2006).

226. Richard Dawkins, *The God Delusion* (Houghton Mifflin, 2006).

227. This statement is attributed to Sam Harris

228. Ken Adelman, "Troubles from Thailand," *The Washington Times*, April 27, 2007, http://www.washingtontimes.com/commentary/20070426-082753-6067r.htm.

229. William Broad, "U.S. is Losing its Dominance in the Sciences," *The New York Times*, May 3, 2004.

230. Staff Reporter, "63% Believe Bible Literally True," *Rasmussen Reports*, April 23, 2005, http://www.rasmussenreports.com/2005/Bible.htm.

231. Julia Oliver, "Graduate Enrollment in Science and Engineering Programs Up in 2003, but Declines for First-

Time Foreign Students," *InfoBrief,* August 2005, http://www.nsf.gov/statistics/infbrief/nsf05317/.

232.Ernie Tretkoff, "Percentage of First-Year Foreign Graduate Students Falls to 43%," *APS.org,* November 2005, http://www.aps.org/publications/apsnews/200511/ foreign-grad.cfm.